Dave & Herman,

My life is so much more
for having you in it!

all you need is GOLF. Fore

Alex

1? June 95

Elegy

for a Golf Pro

Elegy
for a Golf Pro

Dexter Westrum

LYONS & BURFORD, PUBLISHERS

Printed in the United States of America

10 9 8 7 6 5 4 3 2 1

Library of Congress Cataloging-in-Publication Data

Westrum, Dexter.
    Elegy for a golf pro / Dexter Westrum.
        p.   cm.
    ISBN 1-55821-368-6
    1. Westrum, Dexter.   2. Golfers—United States—Biography.
3. Fathers and sons—United States—Case Studies.   I. Title.
GV964.W47A3   1994
796.352'092—dc20
    [B]   94-24363
                                                             CIP

For
Mom and Dad
and
Jane Ann

Contents

Prologue

In 1958 my father and Wally Ulrich stood on the first tee of the Keller Golf Club. They were waiting to play a practice round the Wednesday before the St. Paul Open. Arnold Palmer walked up, his driver in the crook of his arm. That spring he had captured America's heart when he won his first Masters. He looked like the all-American boy, fresh-faced, taut and lean, with a blacksmith's shoulders and forearms.

"You gonna play, Wally?" he asked.

Ulrich nodded. "C'mon along," he said.

"I was gonna ask if I could go out ahead of you," Palmer said, and they laughed. My father, who was standing off to the side of the tee, smiled.

Ulrich introduced my father to Palmer. Palmer asked my father where he was from and what sort of club job he had.

And so they teed off on the 1st hole.

After the second shots, Palmer's caddie put his club away without cleaning it. "You've got to keep these clubs clean," Palmer said to him.

My father gave the boy a tee so he could clean the grooves of Palmer's clubs.

The boy had sold the most season tickets to the St. Paul Open and had got the first choice of pros to caddie for. Of course, he chose Palmer. Actually, the boy really didn't know anything about golf.

I heard later that Palmer fired the boy after the first day of the tournament because he couldn't worry about his game and watch out for the boy, who didn't know what he was doing, at the same time. I don't know if that is really what happened.

I do know that in the middle of the 2nd fairway, while they were walking to their drives, my father introduced me to Arnold Palmer.

Palmer shook my hand and didn't let go of it for a whole minute. "My dad is a golf pro," he said.

"Um hum," I said, shaking my head up and down, trying to let him know that I already knew that.

"You be a good boy and help your father," he said.

In a few holes we had a rather large gallery. An elderly, knobby-kneed man who was wearing a tan cap with a duck-billed see-through green visor came over and put his face near my ear.

"I recognize the other two," he said. "But who is that one, the one over there?" He held a crooked finger generally in the direction of my father.

"That's my old man," I said. "He's a golf pro."

Elegy

for a Golf Pro

1

Hands through the Ball

My father died three years ago. He was a small-town golf pro with a restless soul who could never live in one place very long. He was a working pro, often combining the duties of golf pro with club manager or greenskeeper. I could never understand why we had to move all the time, but I came to believe it had everything to do with the game itself. Golf is a game as solitary and indefinite as life. When all is said and done, it isn't the score that really matters, and surely, it does not matter whether you beat anybody, because you don't play people, you play the course; but it does matter whether you come off the course with your integrity and your dignity in tact. What is important is whether you have submitted your soul to the game. I think my father may have come to feel that, and I think he believed in the existence of a place where everyone subscribed to the same notion. He felt he had only to keep moving, and sooner or later he would wind up there.

The first job I actually remember my father holding was that of fireman. I remember when I was a very small boy I would stay overnight at the fire station. Usually a dozen or so firemen were on duty. They took turns cooking. I remember how strange it was to see my father in an apron cooking. His specialty was chipped beef on toast.

Being a fireman was actually a good job for a man who loved golf. My father worked every other day in twenty-four hour shifts so he had every other day to play golf. Whether he played well or not, he had a steady salary, medical benefits, and a retirement plan. I think he had it made, but my father didn't see it that way. He thought being a fireman kept him from being a true golf professional; he could not be a fireman and live out his destiny in the game.

I learned the golf business from my father, who was a much better player than I ever will be, but I failed to learn how to listen to the game itself. I failed to understand that my father found in golf the rhythms of life. I miss my father because I think I learned too late what the game meant to him, and I would like to see him for just one more afternoon on the golf course, a leisurely nine holes, so I could let him know that I think I might just now understand him.

Unlike my father, I am strictly a teaching pro. I don't have to make a large portion of my income by stocking and selling golf merchandise. I don't have to organize and run golf events. I really don't even have to get along with the club members. I work for a head pro. Head pros are usually too busy to give lessons, so they hire guys like me to do the teaching. Sometimes we also work in the pro shop, but we don't invest in the inventory. Sometimes we are 1st-tee starters, but we don't have to play politics with the members. We follow the rules; our job doesn't depend on playing favorites.

Unlike my father, I have never sought to ply my trade in small towns. I work in big cities, at expensive clubs, where most of the members can afford to go first class. They treat me like a professional, like a person who knows his craft, and I treat them like people who have worked hard to become the successes they are. We aren't interested in being friends. I don't expect them to like me or feel they know me just because I work at the club.

In my youth, it was competitive golf that held my greatest interest. Not only my career in golf, of course, but my father's. He played regularly in sectional championships and regional tournaments and even took a couple of swings on the Tour. He was never much of a sensation, but he did win an occasional pro-am, and now and then he would win money by finishing high in an obscure tournament like the North Dakota Open. Like most club pros, he was lucky to play his own golf course once a week, so I don't really think he saw himself as a dominant player, although he understood that he could get hot and finishing in the money certainly wasn't out of the question.

My earliest memories are of carrying his clubs to the car when he was getting ready to leave for a tournament. As I set his bag in the backseat, I would run my hands over the irons, still hot from washing, and instruct them to hit the ball close to the hole all day. My father would always be a few steps behind me, his hands occupied with a carryall and a single sportcoat on a hanger. His relaxed amble barely disguising a pre-tournament anxiousness, he would say, "Take care of things." Without looking back, he would drive off. I would stand in the parking lot of whatever country club we were working at until he was out of sight.

My hope was that he would play respectably—something in the mid-70s or better so he could come home and face the club members, who I was sure put undue pressure on "their pro." I had this idea because the very first professional tournament I remember my father playing in was the St. Paul Open in 1957. He had played in other St. Paul Opens, but it wasn't until I reached the age of twelve that I became aware of what exactly it was that my father did, and it was the tournaments that captured my imagination, not the daily life of the pro shop, to which I became more or less chained that year.

The St. Paul Open was a full-fledged tour stop in those days, and all the big names—Sam Snead, Doug Ford, Arnold

Palmer—were there. I think I actually thought my father could go up and play the touring professionals even. I somehow thought club professionals and touring pros were in the same business. I was also somewhat smug about what my father did. He didn't work in an office or a factory like the other dads I knew. He had a unique skill; often, because he preferred the pace of life in the rural backwaters, he was the only golf pro in town. And I was the golf pro's kid.

So in 1957 my father had gone up to the St. Paul Open to play with the big hitters, and I stayed home tending the pro shop all by myself. Word came back from someone who had gone up to watch the first day that "their pro" had opened with an 83. Not much of a score, even on a tough course, and the St. Paul Open was played at Keller Golf Club, regularly cut to ribbons by the touring pros. That year Ken Venturi won with something like 20 under par for 72 holes, and here was my father 11 over on the first eighteen.

I was crushed, and to make matters worse, I had to listen to a Joe Blow of a club member get on the old man's case. He was a tall man with receding curly hair and long, muscleless arms. He used the pay phone on the pro-shop wall to call all his buddies one at a time. "Did you hear what our pro did?" He seemed to camp on "our pro" as if the notion were the most ridiculous thing he had ever heard. "83. Some pro. 83. Can you believe it? We'll have to give him strokes."

Joe Blow ran a clothing store downtown. The old man could beat him a hundred times in a row. I couldn't see that he had any license to enjoy the old man's bad luck. I suppose

Joe Blow, content with his small-town existence, felt the old man was overreaching himself to enter the St. Paul Open. Joe Blow just didn't understand golf pros. I didn't understand golf pros either back then, but I still saw Joe Blow as an enemy, a serious danger to the sanctity of my father's opinion of himself.

The next day the old man shot a 71 and, even though he missed the 36-hole cut, restored his dignity somewhat. But that didn't change my response to the clothier. I resolved immediately to grow up to be a pro myself. I would beat practice balls, each one bearing Joe Blow's loud-mouthed face, for a hundred years if need be so that I could grow up and win the St. Paul Open, and then I would come back to his clothing store, stick my championship face in his ugly puss, and ask him how many strokes he was going to give *me*.

My trying so hard to become a player in those early years left a kind of gap between my father and me. I disappointed myself so much that my father came to believe that the only thing I valued was good playing. My frustration with myself became a kind of pressure that he put on himself.

Around the time I was twenty, we were working a club in South Dakota, and my father had left me in charge while he competed in the Minnesota State Open. The morning after the first round, I jumped out of bed and, even before breakfast, raced to a local café to buy a *Minneapolis Tribune*. I stood in the street and read the scores. I was crushed; the old man was nearly dead last with an 83. I couldn't understand it.

Just two years before, he had shot 72 and taken second in a one-day event on the same course.

Shortly after lunch my father returned to the shop. That he was home before dark told me he hadn't stayed to repair his dignity with a decent score in the final round but had elected instead to withdraw. He looked exhausted, his shoulders stooped, his mouth down at the corners.

As I helped him put his gear away, I asked him who was leading when he left and if he'd talked to this old friend or that. He answered matter-of-factly. I knew sooner or later I would have to hear about his round, probably all 83 shots, so I said, "I was hoping you would play well."

He turned and looked at me and immediately started shouting. "You hoped. You hoped! All I ever do is play for you. It doesn't make a damn bit of difference how hard I try."

I tried to stand up to him. I told him that when I said I was hoping for him, that's exactly what I meant. I wasn't asking him to play for me. I stammered, the words all coming out on top of themselves. "Who in hell am I supposed to hope for?" My chest ached. "You're my father, for Christ's sake."

He stood there with his mouth open, and I started to cry.

"It's all right," he said. "Why don't you take the rest of the day off. Go out and play or something."

"I don't have to go play," I said.

He had a couple of small cigars in his shirt pocket, the kind with the white plastic tips. He took them out and said,

"Well, how about a cigar then?" He held both of them out toward me.

I just looked at him, and then I started to laugh. "What the hell am I going to do with a cigar?"

He looked at the cigars, puny in their cellophane between his pudgy fingers, and he started to laugh.

Up until that moment I had thought that I was trying to please him. Since I knew by then that I would not become a tournament player, I already felt that I was the one who had failed. I had made more than my share of trips home from high school matches, wondering how I would explain my horrendous scores. I usually said the same things to him that he said to me. "I hit it like gangbusters, but I just couldn't putt," or "I was paired with a guy that couldn't hit his hind end with a mirror and I couldn't concentrate."

My father, a good player, simply tried too hard. And that is a great sadness because he had the shots, he could make the ball do what he wanted, and he was an excellent head-to-head money player. I, on the other hand, tried too hard because I simply didn't have the shots. I tried to shoot scores in tournaments and matches on strange courses that I couldn't shoot for fun on my own course. Without the shots you don't develop.

Three years before the South Dakota explosion, the old man was associate professional at a course in St. Paul. As a favor, the head professional put me on staff repairing clubs and picking up balls on the practice range. I had hoped that a summer on a big-city course would mature my game, but by early August, if anything, I had gotten worse. One afternoon my father worked with me on the range and deduced my problem as a failure to get the hands through the ball. One thing all good golfers have is strong hands. I had lazy hands. Rather than lead the club through the shot, my hands quit at impact and passively rode the club through the swing.

Once I hit a few good shots, the old man suggested we play the front nine before dark. On the 5th hole, a short 5 par to an elevated green, I drove into thick rough. Even though the ball was trapped, I attempted to hit a 3-wood, and thanks to my uninspired hands, moved the ball a scant five feet. Immediately thunder struck behind me. "Oh my God. I don't know why I try." The old man dropped his clubs on the fairway and stood bent at the knees, a bear ready to pounce, as if he could scare good shots out of me. "Sometimes I just wish you'd plan to grow up and sell shoes." We played the final four holes in a silence not even broken on the 9th hole when I hit a 6-iron out of thick rough to within a foot of the pin for an easy birdie, which allowed me to finish one over par—my best ever on that particular nine.

Because of his illness my father hardly played during the decade before he died. The last time we played, twelve or thirteen years ago, his disease simply would not allow him to release the power in his hands and legs. All he could do was saw at the ball with his arms. Once one of the longest drivers around, he barely managed to get the ball 200 yards from the tee. He couldn't get his fairway woods up; his pitches would stray from the target. He stood this humiliation for four or five holes and then he simply exploded. He groused about every swing, slamming woods into the ground and tossing irons after errant shots. It had been a couple of years since I had played with him and I was not prepared for the demise of his game. I couldn't possibly try to say anything that would help, and I couldn't watch what fate had done to my father.

I went numb, wishing I hadn't come. A shot or two of my own went sour, and soon he started in on me. "You never learned to use your hands," he said and let out a breath like he'd been kicked in the stomach. "It was like talking to a wall. How can you take money from people for lessons when you can't hit the ball out of your shadow?" He took a swipe at a 6-iron approach, which dribbled and hopped thirty or so feet in front of him. "Ah, the hell with it," he said, flinging the club end over end into the deep rough.

He knew enough to parlay this hack-and-roll golf into scores in the low 80s, scores that most people who play golf regularly would envy. But that wasn't enough. He had allowed the need to score to get the better of him. His whole sense of self-worth rode on today's round, on the last shot. There could be no such thing as a past master: you are either a good player, or you are not. There is no face-saving irony or humor when people try too hard. He was no longer a master; his game was gone. And the final degradation was that he had to demonstrate his demise in front of the person he had always tried the hardest to play for, me.

During the summer when he had been an associate pro

in the Twin Cities, my father played in almost every sectional tournament he could get to. He was really looking for a head pro's job since the associate's position brought in only enough money for him to support himself. My mother and sister maintained our home in southern Minnesota, where my mother worked as a secretary. It was late September; I no longer worked at the golf course, but was home for my senior year in high school. The old man was playing a one-day event in a nearby town and planned to stay overnight with us before returning to St. Paul.

Something jarred me awake in the middle of the night, and I sat straight up. The light was on, and the golf pro stood in the doorway wearing the biggest shit-eating grin of his life. "I won it all, junior, I won it all." I blinked and then noticed I'd been joined in bed by a roll of bills easily two inches thick and held together by a wide rubber band. He turned off the light, and I fell back asleep. In the morning the roll of bills still lay beside me.

At breakfast he told us what happened. He had shot the course in four under to win the low-pro prize, and his team (the teams are composed of a visiting pro and three local amateurs of various handicaps) had won the low-team prize. He handed mother the winning checks for the two divisions. "But what about the roll of bills?" I wanted to know. Through another grin almost as big as the one the night before, he said, "I had the only win ticket on my team. That roll is almost fifty percent of the total pari-mutuel pot."

This victory was not just a great day in my father's

career as a minor tournament player, but a vindication of him as a man. It had been six years since he left his fireman's job to turn pro. He had really not found himself cut out for the public-relations aspect of country-club life, nor had he developed a name for himself as a tournament player. To make matters worse, at the age of forty-two, with two children to raise, he had found himself unable to find a head professional position. My mother's job kept us together while he pursued his dream. He felt, I'm sure, that we all thought he was chasing that dream at our expense. And so, the conquering hero returned to the hearth with several hundred dollars—not a bad haul in 1962 money. For a brief moment my father could ease the pressure he put on himself because of what he thought were my expectations. I say "my expectations" because I was the only one he woke up with the news. Everyone else had to wait until morning.

2

At the Top of the Swing

When I was a kid, I was so wrapped up with golf that I didn't have my first great love affair until I was in high school. Nancy Holmes, who was a sophomore when I was a junior, would come out to the club and play golf with her giggly, chatty friends in the mornings when the grass was still wet and glaring in the sun. I would watch her from the pro-shop door while she putted out on number 6 and walked to the 7th tee, which was on the other side of the clubhouse. There was a drinking fountain in front of the pro shop and she would stop there. I was close enough to see water drops on her chin.

She knew I was looking at her. When she lifted her head, she would look at me from the corner of her eyes. Her eyes were her best feature. They were large and brown going on black. Brown-eyed women make me feel like I do when I hit the ball in the middle of the club face, like I was born for this moment.

Nancy was small boned; she had golden blonde hair and a tan she'd worked at. She didn't hit the ball very well. In those days we would have said she swung like a girl. She left all her power in the backswing and daintily dropped the club on the ball. The ball would squirt off and she would giggle.

Sometimes I thought my old man wasn't real happy being a golf pro. He complained a lot about how things weren't like they were in the old days. In the old days people bought all their golf equipment from the pro. They didn't get everything from discount houses in Minneapolis. We had a lot of members who wouldn't even buy tees from our shop. "I remember once when Mac Dunhill had a member who showed up with a set of clubs he got from somewhere else," my old man said. Mac Dunhill was the golf pro who got my old man started in the game back in the thirties. "He tried to put 'em in Mac's club storage. 'You put 'em in here and you'll never see 'em again,' Mac told him. 'You wouldn't do that,' the guy said. Soon as the guy was gone, Mac looked at me and said, 'Young man, take that set of clubs down to number 7 slough and throw them as far in as you can.' "

The old man had a million stories like that. They always ended the same. Mac always shamed the member into living up to his responsibility and buying his equipment from the home pro. If the old man was right, those must have been the greatest days that club professionals ever lived.

I was still just a teenager when I realized the old man was his own problem. He used to take these small-town jobs where he'd have to make half his money in sales, and then he'd stock a pro shop like he was in some big club in Minneapolis. "People just don't know what it means to belong to a country club," the old man loved to say. Actually, there weren't but three or four members in the whole town who could outfit themselves the way the old man thought you should to play the game. "Have you ever thought of not buying so much?" I once asked, my voice barely clearing my lips. "There's good money in balls and gloves and tees." The old man looked at me blankly. He picked a 9-iron off a display rack and stroked the carpet as if he were chipping. "The markup in clubs isn't all that hot," I said. "Everybody wants to trade their old clubs. You've got all kinds of money tied up in used clubs."

He placed the 9-iron back on the display rack. "You can't sell it if you don't have it," he said.

At the end of every summer, he'd have half the shop left, and we'd have to truck it home for the winter. Sets of used irons lined the backs of closets; putters and wedges by the many dozens gathered dust in corners.

I didn't really care much about that end of the business because I wanted to play the Tour. And so the summer of Nancy Holmes, I mostly worried about how well I was hitting the ball. I spent all the time I could on the course or the practice tee.

One day I spoke to Nancy Holmes. I was already at the drinking fountain when she and her friends came up on 6. I watched her take eight to get down from the sand trap. I held the water for her when she walked over to get a drink. Her friends didn't drink. They walked halfway to 7 tee and then turned and watched us. They giggled. "You guys don't play very well," I said. "I could show you how to hit that sand shot."

"I can't hit any shots," she said. The skin turned white on her knuckles as she smeared water drops into her chin.

"I can hit all the shots," I said. I couldn't, of course. But I'd been listening to my old man talk about his golf game for so long I had learned the conversation without learning the skill.

One day it rained and we closed the pro shop early. When I found myself at home in the evening with nothing to do, I walked out to the Holmes house. They lived in a cream-colored stucco house that was covered with vines and had a backyard that fell away to the shores of Fountain Lake. Our house was huge, too, only it was on the north side by the packing plant. We rented. Nancy's father was a C.P.A. who sported a below-the-belt bulge and who was treasurer for the country club. He was surprised to see me.

Nancy and I sat out on her front steps and I asked her if she wanted to learn how to hit all the shots. "I don't think golf is something you're supposed to be good at if you're a girl," she said.

"Oh no?" I said. "Babe Didrikson was one of the best golfers that ever lived." I started to tell her about the time my old man caddied for the Babe. When he was young she played an exhibition in the old hometown when Mac Dunhill was teaching the old man to be a golf pro. On one hole he told her she needed a 5-iron to reach the green, and she said, "Young man, I'll club myself." She hit a 7-iron into the front bunker. The old man threw down a ball and handed her the 5. She hit it to the center of the green. She didn't smile or anything. She just set her jaw at the old man, and said, "Young man, you may club me for the rest of the round."

I started to tell Nancy about that, but she said, "I was really mad it rained. I wanted to go out to the pool and lay in the sun."

"This was my first half-day off," I said.

"I don't think I'd like a job where I had to work all the time," she said, and then she told me about all the things she had done all day, like shopping and talking on the phone. I don't remember what-all she said, but I remember the way her lips moved. They didn't move evenly as if under one command, but they moved like plump pink caterpillars, humping and rolling. Now and then the point of her tongue would pick a spit bubble off the lower edge of the upper one.

"You know," I said one day to my old man, "I think I'm

swaying at the top of the backswing. I'm not bringing the clubhead in square." I was unpacking a new set of irons some salesman had just left with us. They had dimples in the faces instead of grooves, which was supposed to increase the backspin. Only pros could sell them. They were going to revolutionize the game.

"Practice hitting the ball on one foot," he said. "You'll have to stand still or you'll fall down." The old man was checking to see how many lessons he would have to give. Usually his book was full. Wherever we lived, he had a reputation as a teacher. Especially in the old hometown. I know because every time I visit my mother, she introduces me to yet another octogenarian who can't wait to share fond memories of learning from my father how to swing the club and hit the ball straight. "He was such a patient man on the lesson tee," they say.

I tried to teach Nancy Holmes, but it was hopeless. Back then I didn't know that you had to work with people's natural rhythms. I tried to teach her to swing the same way I did. She was small like a bird, and I was a big lump. The balls just squirted off left and right, and hardly ever got into the air. What I did like, though, was touching her. "Golf pros get to touch people," I said. "So don't jump." I remember squaring her fragile shoulders with my open palms, and working the soft rubber behind her knees with my thumbs. "You've got to relax at the point of address," I said.

Mostly she just giggled and laughed. "You're fun," she said. She didn't really care if she could hit the ball or not.

"Let's try putting up on the practice green," I said after I realized she would never get the ball into the air.

I missed the best shot my old man ever hit, and what galls me is that I could have seen it. He had gone up to Minneapolis to play in the State Open, which was televised. But the only TV at the club was in the bar. Legally, I couldn't go in the bar because I was only fifteen. That Sunday I went in anyway and got the tournament on the set. The pro shop was next to the bar and I sort of hung in the doorway, keeping an eye on the threesomes as they finished. In those days the local stations limited their coverage to the final hole. I saw a number of players come and go, but I had yet to see my father's bearlike gait.

Slowly I worked my way from the doorway to the end of the bar. From there I could actually hear the set. Then some member saw me and squeaked up: "What's that kid doing in here? Get that kid out of here. We could lose our liquor license." Nancy's father was the only board member in the clubhouse at the time so the crowd prevailed on him to usher me back to the pro shop.

Nancy's old man was not a bad guy, really. He was just an accountant; he liked things to proceed in an orderly way. Once when we were first at the club—before my father got mad at everybody because they wouldn't buy all the equipment he stocked—I heard Nancy's father talking about a basketball game he had played in as a high school kid. It was the big game against their archrivals and the score was tied. Every time some guy tells a story like this, it's always the big game against their archrival and the entire well-being of the town depends on what happens. The score was tied with a second to play, and Mr. Holmes had passed in from out of bounds to his best buddy, the local superstar, and the superstar had scored as the buzzer rang. They would be heroes forever. But the referee disallowed the basket because he said he hadn't tapped the ball before Mr. Holmes passed it in. The ruling stuck and Mr. Holmes was still very sad about it. In fact, he felt incomplete.

But he was not sad when he talked to me. He was stern. He didn't care that I wanted to see my old man on television. The law said I was not to be in the bar. When I kept protesting, he hit me with something I didn't know anything about.

"You have the same problem your father does. You don't know your place. He's an employee out here. This club was not created just for him to be the gentleman pro."

I couldn't quite understand how he thought he could lay into my old man like that, especially when the old man wasn't even in the room. "Is that right?" I said. "All I know is you people are so cheap if it cost a dime to crap, you'd try to vomit."

"The board's been getting complaints about you, too. Hitting the ball on one foot, showing off to the girls in the swimming pool. What do you think this is, some sort of showboat?"

"I'm trying to learn how to hit the ball so I can get a job in a real country club and not have to be around people like you."

That confused him, but not for long. "I don't think I

want to see you talking to my daughter ever again," he said. "Is that clear?" I guess he thought he'd just wedged in to save par from the tall grass. Somehow denying me his daughter's company would make me feel as perpetually incomplete as he did about losing the big game to the archrival.

When I didn't respond as if my world had ended, he stared at me blankly. The thought that I might have a point of view had honestly not occurred to him. He was doing me a favor by making my place clear to me. I did not understand this concept of place. I knew his place. Mr. Holmes couldn't get it under 100 to save his left foot. I'd shot 38 twice in the last week.

While all this is going on, the old man's threesome is playing the last hole. Only they've been away for a commercial and the coverage doesn't actually start until his playing partners are on the green. But the old man is nowhere to be seen. The announcers are talking among themselves wondering if he's withdrawn. There seems to be no official word. All of sudden a ball comes into the picture. It lands beyond the flagstick, takes one hop, bites, and spins backward to within a few inches of the cup.

The old man had hit his approach shot nearly off the course into a stand of fir trees. In the trees, he had no shot so he'd hit a sand wedge forty feet high straight up out of deep rough and still carried it some fifty yards. And almost holed it.

The old man talked about it for days afterward. "I'm sitting in the middle of all that balsam without a prayer. Got a real fluffy lie. The grass is so long the ball is practically suspended."

Here he would pause so the listener could develop a clear mental picture. "Then I say to myself, 'Hell, you know what to do. Trust the swing.' I open the clubface and let her rip."

There was an article in the Minneapolis paper about how he executed the shot. The conception of the shot is no big deal, of course, to anybody who knows the game, but most of the people who read newspapers don't, so my old man had his day in the sun. And I missed it. I don't remember if he made any money in the tournament, but to this day that clipping is safe in the scrapbook at my mother's place.

My exchange with Mr. Holmes was the first time I knew my old man was in hot water at the club. I should have guessed it. We'd been there three years, about as long as we stayed anywhere. Things got worse, and my father agreed to leave, if the club would buy his inventory. Actually, he had an angle on a club in another small town, where he was certain people knew what it meant to be country club members.

The idea of moving again made my mother really sad because she had a good secretary's job in town, and she didn't want to leave. "We never get roots down," she said. "Just like a woman," the old man said. But that wasn't the worst part. The board and the old man couldn't agree on the price. The board wanted to pay fifty cents on the dollar, the old man wanted sixty, his cost. If he didn't get sixty, we ran the risk of having trouble getting through the winter. Staying in town and getting by on my mother's salary was, according to his logic, out of the question.

"I can't bear to go in there and negotiate with those cheapskates," he said. "I'll start throwing punches. I'll tear them apart." He looked at me. "You'll have to get us sixty cents on the dollar."

The week after Labor Day the golf season is pretty well over in Minnesota. Mr. Holmes and I sat at a poker table out on the upstairs porch of the clubhouse on a Sunday afternoon. I had all my father's invoices in a folder and the books, which I'd helped my mother post right up to the end of the season. Mr. Holmes had one of those mechanical pencils all accountants carry, the ones with the extra-long erasers on the ends. I passed him the documents and I watched him read.

After a couple hours, Jerry Offenbecker, the club president, came in. "Isn't this done yet? I thought you were going to be like the army and get this over with fast." Mr. Offenbecker had a golf-ball nose and the quick showed red around his eyes. He was a big wheel in the chamber of commerce and the Lutheran church. I don't know what he did for a living. He had a store of some sort downtown. He stood over us and rocked back and forth on his heels. "Why is he sending a fifteen-year-old kid to do this?" Mr. Holmes kept reading and didn't answer him.

"Mr. Offenbecker," I said, after a while. "Mr. Holmes and I are doing fine. If you will leave us alone, we will come to an agreement soon." I looked him straight in the eye, and he fidgeted once or twice and left. The only reason I could look him in the eye was that I was imagining how stupid he looked when he swung at the ball. And I was thinking about how much I didn't like him. Both he and his wife swung like shovels and couldn't break a hundred to save cottage cheese.

And they were cheap. Mr. Offenbecker ordered all his equipment through his business, and once Mrs. Offenbecker had fallen in love with a new style of windbreaker we had just stocked. After taking forever to decide which one fit perfectly, she said: "Can I take this one home for Jerry's approval?" I was so thrilled at the prospect of finally selling her something, I agreed. It was a dandy windbreaker, lightweight, powder blue with white trim.

The next day she brought it back. "Jerry doesn't like it." A week after that she appeared in one just like it. "I made this myself, what do you think?" she asked my old man. She had taken ours home to cut a pattern.

Nancy's father passed the documents back at me across the table. "You keep these books?"

"Some," I said. "I log each day, and my mom's teaching me to do the other stuff. She checks everything, but I do a lot."

He looked at me as if he were thinking what to say next. He shot his jaw and scratched his upper lip with his lower teeth. Then he looked out over the golf course. The course was a dull autumn green and the leaves had not started to turn.

"I love to play in the fall," I said. "There are usually not many people around."

"I've never thought of playing after Labor Day," he said. He lifted his pencil up in front of his face and dropped the lead down the barrel. He studied the empty hole before he spoke. "I'm empowered to go to fifty-five cents. I think I'd like to do that."

"That's fine, Mr. Holmes," I said.

He took the official club checkbook out of his pocket and screwed the cap off his fountain pen. "You know, I think it would be all right if you came around to talk to Nancy."

I watched him write the check, which he handed to me across the table. "I mean that," he said.

"Well, we're going to be leaving town, Mr. Holmes," I said. "But you tell Nancy I told you to tell her she's never going to hit the ball if she keeps leaving all her power at the top of the swing."

3

Getting Her Danish Up

For most of her life my mother did what she was told. She was a teenager in the thirties, the oldest child of a strict father, whose own mother was an Indian and whose father had been a rounder who followed the horse-racing circuit. The Indian had thrown pots to keep her family together and her husband, who was actually a gentle but fun-loving man, in gambling money. Grandpa might not have been so strict except he married Grandma, who was a full-blooded

Dane and a Baptist. Grandpa felt daughters should obey without question, and that's what my mother did. She had a 9:30 curfew, for instance, when she was a senior in high school.

The only boyfriend she ever had was my father. They got stuck on each other when they were ninth graders and married when they were in their early twenties. Once when they were in high school a boy from the Baptist church asked my mother to go ice skating, and she went. My father, who was also on the ice, saw them skating along holding hands. An excellent skater who already had some local renown as a hockey player, the old man came in from behind and hip-checked the Baptist boy, who came to rest on his belly with his face in the snow. My mother evidently thought my father's behavior quite a dashing feat because she accepted no more dates from anyone else.

Over the years mother held many office jobs while my father followed his career as a golf professional. My mother's jobs often had more potential than my father's, but hers were always "just temporary, just to help out until things got going for Dad."

Mother was second in her high school graduating class but received no college scholarship offers. My father, a much less impressive student, turned down scholarships for both football and hockey. And in truth, my mother had no options. She was a woman.

Once after I had left home for good, I visited my parents because I wanted the old man to work on my game. The sectional championship was coming up, and I had been told that if I could finish near par I would have a good chance at a winter teaching job at a swank club in Palm Springs. I mostly needed the old man to work with me on the practice range so I could gain confidence in my swing. As a rule, I don't play much, and I hardly ever enter tournaments.

This particular day my father had got it into his head that their phone should ring both at their home and at the pro shop. My mother was calling the phone company with his request. Since the pro-shop phone was a pay phone, the phone company could not accommodate her. Father, listening to her half of the conversation, suddenly exploded. "The devil with them. We don't want their phone here. Tell them to come take it out."

With this volcano exploding beside her, she continued a nervous conversation, trying to work things out. My father arched his back, bent his knees and appeared ready to spring into the phone after whoever this enemy was who was messing up his life; then in a range so high and exasperated it was barely audible, he said, "You promised to obey. Now, hang up that phone."

She hung up the phone.

I marvel at my mother's stamina for daily life. It is some remarkable streak of stubborn resolve, I suppose, that quality my father referred to as "getting her Danish up." But maybe it isn't anything like that at all. Maybe it is simple endurance, the last small garret in the outpost of life.

My mother's "Danish," however, seldom surfaced in confrontations with my father. Her best efforts she reserved for others, like the time she became women's club champion at a course we once worked in South Dakota. My father's various contracts always included playing privileges for his family. My mother's normal procedure was to join the Women's Organization and to play "with the gals" on the day that most clubs set aside as "Ladies Day." The "gals" usually threw quarters into a pot and played for various serious and unserious prizes. Mother played a steady bogey golf on this particular course, respectable, even better than most, but certainly no threat to the championship players of the women's group. After their rounds the women stayed for lunch and cards, everyone generally not being overcompetitive and having a good time.

Because we were never actually members of the club, mother never entered the club championship, which usually climaxed the season. But our last year in South Dakota she was drafted into the club tournament. The championship flight was made up of the women who had the sixteen lowest handicaps. It just happened that the woman with the highest of the lowest handicaps had to drop out of the tournament. The normal procedure would have been to move up the lowest handicap player from the first flight. But this particular year, there were complications.

A new woman had joined the club, a woman taller, stronger, and younger than any of the other good players. She always shot the low score on Ladies' Day and was generally regarded as one of the best women players in the city. Whoever filled the vacant spot in the championship flight would have to play her in the first round. In other words, whoever moved up from the first flight would be a sacrificial lamb.

Nobody wanted the job. The woman whose handicap qualified for the spot was enjoying her first season as a decent player and had her heart set on winning the first-flight cup. She would not consent to being moved up. The tournament committee talked to all the other women in the club whose handicaps also qualified them, but found that they had no interest in the club tournament or they would have entered in the first place.

That left only my mother. Her handicap was perfect, but she wasn't a member. But membership was not a problem—in this case. After all, whoever played against this new taller, stronger, and younger arrival would surely fall—nobody had beaten this woman all year. The first-flight cup would be saved for its rightful "owner" and country-club life could go on as God ordained.

The women's golf committee, however, erred in one significant respect. They assumed my mother would understand the scenario. They didn't understand that my mother was not tuned to the local tournament scene. She played golf because she loved to play golf. She played golf because she loved "the gals." Winning or losing had nothing to do with my mother's approach to the game. She saw it all as some sort of fellowship, some sort of coming together for the fun of coming together. She was honored that "the gals" asked her to play in "their" championship.

And so she went out and played the new arrival and closed her out before the eighteen holes were over. What none of us knew was that the new arrival choked in tournaments. The new arrival did not understand that she was taller, stronger, and younger than any of the other good woman players. She did not know that she was supposed to win the club tournament without a struggle.

She was, in fact, frightened at having to play the pro's wife. It did not matter that mother's average game was five to ten shots higher than hers, that she could beat my mother's best day ten out of ten times with her own average round. She "took the gas" and played to the high side of her game, and my mother's unassuming bunt-walk-and-enjoy-yourself bogey golf buried her. And the new arrival, good sport that she was, rested in peace.

The remaining members of the championship flight, however, did not rest in peace. They lay awake in fear. Who was this woman who up until now had always had a smile and a good word for everybody, and what had she done? Killed Goliath, nothing less. And so mother played golf, and her opponents fell until she found herself in the finals.

"She doesn't win tournaments," I said to my father at the time. "The prize for nonstop talking on Ladies' Day is more her style."

My father smiled. "She's got her Danish up. They'd better look out."

The other finalist was a sturdy little woman with a compact swing who had never been champion. On a normal day she would edge my mother by a stroke or two. I expected her to put mother away by the 15th hole. When they rounded the turn all even, I began to worry. There had always been an unstated rule that whenever my father or I had had to fill out a foursome in a team event, it was always all right for us to finish second. The club members saw our participation as a bit of a novelty and were glad that Dad or I had been available when a member had been forced to withdraw at the last minute. Team events were fine, but we were never invited or encouraged to enter club events that were decided by individual scores. We were, after all, not members.

On the day of the championship round, the two finalists finished the regulation eighteen even. Both shot even bogeys. I watched from the pro-shop door as they walked to the 1st tee for sudden death. Their lips set in intense purpose, both women were charged with energy and deep in concentration. It was the first time I realized that my mother was capable of competitive spirit. It was also the first time I began to have fears in my stomach that she was indeed going to win the tournament.

The 1st hole was a brief par 3 over deep water. Mother spanked a 7-iron twelve feet from the cup. Her opponent was wide of the green. Her chip left her outside mother; her first putt was short; she was in in four. Mother lagged, tapped in. The new champion. Senator George McGovern sent her congratulations, and her picture was on the sports page.

At the awards dinner she accepted the cup and thanked the Women's Organization for inviting her to play in "their" championship. She also thanked my father for teaching her to play golf, one of the greatest joys of her life. Some of the audience applauded, some did not. I noticed particularly that a number of the husbands of contestants sat glumly by. My mother's sincere demeanor and humble manner were not enough. My father's contract for the next year contained clauses he could not accept—mother was to quit her job in the club business office and I was not to be employed by the club in any manner—and he resigned. Mother's affront to the ladies pushed us through the thin ice to which my father's natural contentiousness had already brought us.

My parents couldn't afford a moving company, so their goods left town in a cattle truck borrowed from one of the members. I looked at our household huddled between manure-spattered slats, and said where only my mother could hear me, "What are we doing in the golf business anyway? This is one rotten way to live." She took me by the shoulders, which wasn't easy for her to do because she had all she could do to stand as high as my chin. Her eyes never left mine, and she shook me until I felt myself coming apart in the joints. "Don't you ever feel sorry for yourself. Nobody's hurt you. It won't always be this way."

Toward the end of their working lives, my parents shared a position at a country club in northern Minnesota. Mother managed the pro shop and the old man supervised the greens crew and gave lessons. This country club was different in that it was owned by a single individual, rather than the combined resources of the entire membership. This individual was a man used to having his own way, and he and my father maintained at best a wary relationship always on the edge of explosion.

And one day the explosion occurred, probably over a piece of straw like when to fertilize or how high to let the rough grow. Undoubtedly the main issue was that each man felt the other didn't realize that he knew nothing about golf courses and should without hesitation do as he was told. So my father stormed into the pro shop and gathered his own clubs and tools and went to the trailer house my parents called home.

My mother finished the day in the shop and upon arriving home was told that they were through with this place. "As far as I'm concerned," the old man rasped, "he can shove his golf course up his nose. Tomorrow I want you to pack this place up. We're going to go out and beat the bushes for another job."

In the morning my father was awakened by kitchen noises. Emerging from the bedroom, his great belly protruding over his shorts, he rubbed enough sleep from his eyes to see mother fully dressed about to leave. "Where you going?" he asked.

"Somebody's got to work," she said.

My father's eyes grew large. "Don't get your Danish up about this," he said. "I said we are leaving. We'll go beat the bushes for another job."

"We don't have any money in the bank," she said. "I'm

too tired to beat the bushes, and I'm too tired to pack this place up."

My mother has a favorite story about her father. It seems when she was a little girl, she had an autograph book, and she asked her father to write in it. I imagine Grandpa, a kind but now and then grouchy man, bemused by his first-born, but at the same time taking the request quite seriously. He took the book and wrote, "Always be a blessing."

4

Turning the Old Man Loose

"Do you think it will be all right?"

My mother sits in the easy chair, I on the couch, one leg up, my shoes off. We are in the living room in the high-rise. There is no light except the bathroom light, which gives mother a sort of blue-gray glow. Her face is round, and if not happy, perpetually hopeful. She has borne my father's death, coming as it did after years of suffering, as a release, for him, for her. "It is what he wanted," she says. "But it is against the law in Minnesota."

My sister sits at what would be the kitchen table, except that in my mother's apartment, living room and kitchen are the same. The regulations require them that way if someone is in a wheelchair. Even though my father has died and my mother is not in a wheelchair, the powers that be will allow her to continue to live in this same apartment. Occasionally my sister's cigarette glows orange. The three of us are a triangle of waiting. She answers my mother: "What can they do to us?"

"They could put us in jail," my mother answers with characteristic earnestness.

"They'd have to feed us," my sister says.

My sister is an actress. She does regional theater mostly, in places like Minneapolis, Kansas City, and Cleveland, but has appeared in a couple of films and quite a few commercials. I think she gets a lot of work in commercials because she's built stocky like Dad. She's not fat really, just formidable. She looks like the kind of ordinary person who would be so interested in laundry detergents that really worked that she actually would have to tell someone about them.

Although I've seen these commercials, I've never seen her act on stage. We aren't exactly close, although we certainly don't dislike each other. We are seven years apart, and my parents always liked to say that they raised two "only" children.

My father's ashes sit on the coffee table between us. My mother says they are in a cardboard urn. I don't see the difference between it and a cardboard box. But mother won't discuss the difference because our task is too important to be hindered by quibbling.

I remember a day before he got real bad, before his mind started to go, and my parents explained cremation as the cheaper alternative. He sat in the special thrusting chair the public health service had given him, to help him stand up after long hours of watching television, his last pretense toward life. His once-formidable arms and legs looked like the sort of toothpicks you can't count on not to break. His gray eyes were watery and the old fire just couldn't get started. "Spread me out on the golf course," he said, as if he were telling someone to keep the right elbow in on the backswing.

His legs were useless by then and he hadn't played for three years, but he hadn't given up thinking he would be playing again soon. "I'll get me one of those hotshot doctors at Mayo. There's a procedure. They clean out the veins and I'll get the blood back in my legs and I'll be playing golf again."

I had heard that before. He'd been to the Vets Hospital, he'd been to the University of Minnesota, he'd been everywhere he could talk mother into driving him. The resident gurus in white always ran several days' worth of tests, and they always told him the same thing. The procedure wouldn't work on him. He should go home and make himself walk every day. Who knew what might happen. What they didn't tell him was that he was dying of diabetes, that it would be slow, steady, gruesome, and that not soon enough it would be final.

I don't think even on the day he died he let himself understand that it would be final. "You remember," I say to my mother, "how even at the end he kept talking about moving up to North Dakota? He kept saying how they had some good golf courses up there and how there weren't a lot of people."

"We lived a lot of places," she says without judgment. "The next place was always going to be better. I don't think he knew after a while what it was he was looking for."

I looked around Ma's living room. Her desk, the coffee table, a chair across from me against the wall, all looked blue-gray. "You don't have your club championship trophy out," I said.

Ma laughed. "Been in the closet for years. All the trouble it caused. Sometimes I wish I'd never even seen the dang thing."

"Oh, now, Ma," I said. "That was your day in the sun. And don't you go throwing that thing away. I'm going to want that someday."

My mother took the frown off her face. If the trophy mattered to me, she would allow it to matter to her. "Okay," she said.

Ma still won a lot of prizes, but she didn't play championship golf anymore. She played on ladies' day at the public golf course in the old hometown. We could just as easily have taken the old man's ashes out there and spread them around. Nobody would have objected. He played his last golf on that course. Everybody knew him. They watched his game and mind fall apart and felt the end of a local treasure. We could have spread the old man out in broad daylight and probably drawn a crowd.

But my mother thought it had to be the country club.

Three times he had returned to this club, the last time as greenskeeper. A new syndicate of owners had hired him for one year to train a young kid they planned to employ permanently. The old man was finally in hog heaven. He didn't have to work, but drew a regular check for passing on what was in his head.

But he could not hit the ball. The old procedure of going back to the practice tee and starting all over again hadn't worked this time. The fundamentals of golf could not overcome diabetes. He would stay at the range for hours flailing at balls so fiercely he would fall down. His legs worthless, he would jam his club into the ground and pull himself hand over hand up the shaft. His body was failing him, the game of his life was failing him, and when they would come and try to encourage him to take it easy, he would accuse his friends of failing him.

It was April. The snow was gone, but Minnesota summer was a long way from full force. We didn't need to worry about a night watchman, so I drove right into the parking lot. Everything was quiet. The clubhouse was dark. We sat for a minute.

"Ever wonder what would have happened if he had stayed an amateur and played all his golf here and let it go at that?"

"It wasn't so much the playing," she said. "It was the game itself. It was the one thing other than us that mattered the most. He didn't want to share golf with a job. The job and golf had to be the same. There wasn't a day I knew him that he didn't want to be a golf professional. He idolized the pros he worked for when he was a caddie. They always let him work in the shop, you know. He was the one kid that was really interested."

"You don't think he wanted to play the Tour?" I said.

"No," she said. "He played in a lot of tournaments and disappointed himself many times."

"But he played all right quite a bit of the time."

"He had a chance to go on tour," my mother said. "When Slip-on-Grip sent Wally Ulrich on Tour back in the early fifties, it wasn't just for him to play, you know," she said. "He was supposed to introduce the grip to the tour players and take care of everyone's grips."

"Who is Wally Ulrich?" my sister asked.

"He was a friend of Daddy's," my mother said.

"Before your time," I said. "One of the few Minnesotans who ever won a tournament on the PGA tour."

"I guess that's a big deal, huh?" my sister said.

"Wally came over to see Dad," my mother continued. "Slip-on-Grip thought they should have two people doing the job and they wanted Wally to find somebody else. He wanted Dad to do it. Sat right in our living room and explained the whole thing. I heard it."

My old man was at the top of his game then. I almost blurted out, "He should have gone," but instead, I asked Ma, "What did you think about it?"

"I told him he could make up his own mind," she said.

"So he didn't go," I said.

"No," she said. "I didn't think he would. You were little and it wasn't enough money for us all to travel. He was never one to be away from home for very long."

"I remember that," I said. "The two years he went out on the Winter Tour, he came home way before he said he was going to. One time I got a postcard saying 'It's on to the Texas Open.' I look up from reading the card and there he is pulling into the driveway."

"Well, he really couldn't afford to have been out there, then," she said. "He mostly gave lessons at driving ranges. He didn't tell us that's what he was doing because he didn't want us to worry."

"Well, Ma," I said. "I guess we have to do it."

We got out of the car and slowly walked around the sleeping pro shop, which huddled in the crisp, fresh night, its work about to begin for another summer. I remembered miserable summer afternoons in the club storage room, which wasn't air-conditioned or insulated against southern-Minnesota humidity, and the long evenings of waiting for the couples who would come out after supper and play four holes before dark. They had nothing better to do, and I guess they assumed I had nothing better to do than wait for them so I could wash the mis-hits off their clubs.

"Boy, I don't remember much about this place," my sister said.

"You never were as excited about golf as your brother," my mother said, her earnestness balancing what has to be the greatest understatement of our family life. My sister certainly never did warm to the charms of golf. She was never one to enjoy the pro shop, and after a couple of half-hearted summer stints as a club waitress, she has continued to refer to all club members everywhere, without qualification, as "that bunch of dorks." Since leaving home, she has never gone near a golf course or a country club, a fact in which she takes inordinate pride.

Neither I nor my parents have ever been to my sister's apartment in New York City. "It's too small for company," my sister says. And it probably is. According to her, she has to fold up her kitchen counter to uncover her bathtub.

I do like my sister's attitude, though. She doesn't let people get her down. When the members get to me, which they do more and more, I escape to the club repair bench and brood and putter around until I get over it and can take up my role as the jovial teaching assistant, "who really can't play a lick, but seems to know an awful lot about the game."

My sister doesn't retreat; she gets even. A couple of summers ago, she got a last-minute call from a producer she knows to do Shakespeare in summer stock at the Dorset Playhouse in Vermont. The guy was desperate and he could pay her more than he was paying the other actors, but the part was Ophelia in *Hamlet*. Not exactly a perfect fit for a full-bodied woman who sells a lot of laundry detergent.

I guess there's a place where the character goes crazy and does a little dance. My sister is graceful. Fixed up in a loose night gown and with the proper lighting, she got away with it most nights. But one night as she's just finishing her dance, she hears this gruff voice say, "Nice ankles," meaning, of course, "a little thick on the hoof there."

A quick dart of the eyeballs tells her the offender is a local hardware-store owner. She doesn't tell a soul she has heard this guy. She simply waits.

On the night of the last performance, which is also the final night of the season, she strikes. Leaving the village at four in the morning, she parks her VW Bug at the hardware store. First she encounters the guy's blue-and-white Chevy sport-van. With four deft turns of a bobby pin, she deflates all the tires. Then, with bright-red scenery paint, she writes across the display window, "Why is Hardware Hank so happy?" and underneath adds the name of a well-known massage parlor and strip joint across the line in New York state.

Beyond the clubhouse was the swimming pool, and beyond that, the 7th tee, the highest point on the course. You could see pieces of the play on six of the holes from there. There was a slight breeze. The golf course was a blue-gray. I had shot my first par round here. I was fifteen and the 35 had appeared almost effortlessly amid a summer of 38s and 39s. I was sure I would be a player. It was during the old man's second stint as pro in the old hometown. This particular stay lasted three years.

While I'm thinking about my old scores, my sister wanders over to the swimming pool. With one hop, she is halfway up the chain-link fence surrounding the pool. She leans over backward and looks at my mother and me upside down. My mother ignores her, still, I think, silently fretting about whether or not this is the right thing to do, or the right place to do it. I put my arm across her shoulders. My sister speaks in a hammy stage whisper, "If it were done, 'tis best it were done quickly."

It was all rather anticlimactic really. I didn't ask my mother what she was thinking. Instead, I saw a ten-year-old boy, his face full of the wonder of new information, standing in a kitchen at the beginning of the Depression, telling his mother that he had been out to the golf links that day. His mother, a thick Scandinavian woman, sat rather bemused, a stray strand of hair caught in the sweat on her forehead, her pudgy hands continuing to knead the bread dough in front of her. He had carried a man's golf bag that day and the man had given him a quarter, which was pretty good because he didn't have to give him any more than a dime. It was called caddying. There was a bunch of kids that caddied and a guy called the pro had told him he could be a good caddie if he would work at it, but he would have to come out to the golf links every day, especially on the weekends. On Monday mornings, the caddies could play. He thought he might like this golf. You played it with a ball and a club and you tried to get the ball into a hole. It looked like a game he could play.

With my free hand, I lifted the flaps on the box and held it up to turn the old man loose. A thin sheet of ashes caught the breeze and headed out toward the 7th green.

5

Playing with My Old Man's Clubs

Sonny O'Brien stopped hitting balls as I walked onto the practice tee. "Sorry to hear about your dad," he said.

I dropped my father's clubs on the ground. "Thank you, Sonny," I said. "He was real bad at the end. He's better off now." He pursed his lips and nodded and I could see he was having trouble with tears. He had saved his grief until he saw me.

I had always liked Sonny. A terrier of an Irishman with

a rubber-ball red nose, he had been part of the scene for as long as I could remember. I don't think he ever took a head-pro job. He was always somebody or other's assistant, and he didn't stay in one place for very long. He loved the camaraderie of the pro-ams in the fall, and he didn't care that he seldom played well and rarely got paid. He and Dad had been paired together in a lot of state opens. Sonny must have been nearly seventy by now, and here he was warming up for today's pro-am, probably for the same reason I was, knowing he wasn't necessarily going to play well but hoping that a good warm-up would keep things from getting embarrassing.

Once when I was just barely out of high school, I ran into Sonny when I was playing the last hole of the State Assistant Pros Championship. He had finished his round and was walking down the rough, going out to watch my uncle Thump play the last few holes. Thump was involved in a tussle for the championship with Harold Blaine, a hair-combing hot dog out of Texas. Sonny asked me how many over I was. It had been a long, painful day. "A basketful," I said. He wanted me to be more specific. I told him.

"You birdie this hole and you'll get paid," he said, his voice rising with its usual enthusiasm.

The last hole was a par 5. "I already hit this ball three times," I told him, "and I've got a 5-iron to the green." I held the sole of the club up where he could read the number.

Sonny turned his head back to look at the green, a still-lush carpet in the thick of early October. "A 5 will put you in the clubhouse. Hit 6."

I changed clubs. The ball bounced once on the fringe and settled down into a smooth roll dead on line with the flagstick and disappeared into the cup at the back of the green. I and two other guys split last money.

Uncle Thump's name really wasn't Thump. Dad gave it to him when he taught him how to hit the soft shot. Thump was just a kid then and everybody was amazed at what a natural he was. He played his first nine holes when he was ten years old, and he shot even bogeys. Everybody knew he'd go on to be a champion, and he did. But when he started playing, he couldn't hit the ball very far, so the old man taught him the soft shot.

You hit it with a wide-open sand wedge, the ball off your right heel. You stand open and hit the shot with your wrists. The ball looks like it's going to take off at a low trajectory and go forever, but all of a sudden it just drops with a kind of gentle thump and hardly rolls at all. Your playing partners think you've just skulled your pitch over the green, and thump, there it is by the hole. That was how Thump, when he was just a little kid, managed to save par on the holes that were too long for him to reach in regulation. People got so used to seeing him play the shot, they called him Thump and still do even though when he grew up he hit it as long as anybody.

Thump always liked Sonny. That was the thing about Thump. For a champion he was never haughty or snobbish. Being one of the better players in the section, he was hardly ever paired with Sonny, but he was always happy to see him and always included him when guys went out to dinner at the tournaments and in the gangsomes going round and round the practice green putting for skins.

A lot of the really good players hardly had anything to say to anybody, especially guys like me who were usually not much of a threat. Now and then they might talk to you. You might sit up half the night talking to some almost-but-never-a-major-tour-star like Harold Blaine, hearing all about the woes of his putting or his love life or how he'd lost his card on the big Tour and that was why he was having to hang out with a bunch of club pros; and when you saw him in a week or so at another tournament, he wouldn't remember your name. My dad never let guys get away with that. He'd walk up to them in the locker room and just start talking.

There was never any problem between my dad and Thump either. The old man was fifteen when Thump was born, and he was the one that taught Thump to play. If it bothered Dad that Thump was in some ways the champion he might have wished he was, it never came up. My guess is that such a thought never occurred to him. Or to Thump. I remember once when Thump was Dad's assistant, which he was the first year he was a pro, the old man had just gotten back from a pro-am with the news that he'd finished second. One of the members who happened to be in the shop asked "How'd Thump do?"

"He didn't go," the old man said. "I left him home so

I'd have a chance." Thump was in the shop, too, and just sort of chuckled.

When I'd hit enough balls to be sure the muscles worked, I still had a half-hour before I teed off. So I walked up to the clubhouse to see who was around. Several pros stopped me to shake my hand and say good things about my father. They all had liked him; in the brotherhood of the profession, he had measured up.

Thump was sitting at a corner table in the barroom nursing a cup of coffee. Thump is a head taller than my father, but he has the same blue-gray hair, which falls across his forehead, his golf cap sitting back on his head. My father always had an expectant look in his eye, the sort of look that always asks, What's next? What are you going to do? Thump's eyes are more relaxed. They just kind of take you as you are. And he's almost always smiling. At least he is when he sees me.

I sat down. We compared tee times, but didn't say much. Harold Blaine came in and walked over to us. Blaine has what I call the good-player wiggle. He moves really slow and his shoulders rock. His thin fingers are constantly pulling a bright red foot-long comb through his black hair, which sits in a cold wave above his perpetually suntanned face. Like Thump, he's slender. Unlike Thump, he shows no inclination to add weight around his middle. Neither did he show any inclination to sit, and he seemed not to notice me. "Don't know what you're doing here," he said to Thump. "I'm going to win."

Thump put a smile at the corner of his mouth. "Oh, I can probably take something home," he said. "Should be some fun anyway. Guess we're going to have a derby later."

"I'm going to win it all," Blaine said. He put his comb in his back pocket. Then he looked at me and nudged me in the foot with his toe. "How you doin' this morning?" he asked in his musical drawl.

"I'm doing just fine, Harold," I said, seriously aware of my squashed, chunky self and wishing I had a coffee cup to give my attention to.

"There goes a fan club of one," I said when Harold walked off. He pulled the comb back out of his pocket when he got to the door.

"He's a good player," Thump said. "Frustrated. Can't seem to get through the qualifying school to get back on the Tour. He's old enough to quit dreaming. Won't take a head job. Doesn't want to work."

"Now you've done it," I said. "Just when I was getting ready to despise him for the rest of my life, you give me some reason to feel sorry for him."

"Ahh, don't pay any attention to these guys."

I could just barely remember Thump as a high school kid. While my father's family was traditionally built like teddy bears, Thump was long and gangly. Until he was well into adulthood, his ears were too big for his head. And he always had a golf club in his hand.

Back in the old hometown, my grandparents' house sat

on a hill overlooking the football practice field, and Thump's favorite pastime was to dispose of old golf balls by hitting wood shots out of the front lawn over the football field into the lake that sat in the center of town.

Once when my grandfather, who was a docile and kindly man much like Thump, took objection to this practice, Thump assured him there was nothing to worry about. On the next swing, the ball hit a telephone pole across the street and rebounded into the front of the house, missing a window by an inch. The mark was visible for years. "I didn't say a word and neither did Pa," Thump said. "I just put the club back in the bag and went back in the house."

"So when are you going to settle down?" Thump asked, seemingly out of nowhere. "Aren't you getting tired of keeping your clubs in a different pro shop every season?" My wandering had always seemed strange to Thump. I think he thought I should have seen from my father's example the pointlessness of endless roving.

"I should go out and putt a bit," I said, starting to get up.

"You got time to sit a bit," Thump said in an unusually commanding voice. He got up and went over to the hospitality table and poured me a cup of coffee. When he set it down in front of me, he said, "You should stop bumming around."

"Well, I sure don't want to become a head pro and have to be at the beck and call of club members," I said.

"It doesn't have to be a country club. Get a public

course job. Boy, that was a mistake your dad made. Public course players are just easier to get along with. Mostly they're just working people."

"Doesn't sound too glamorous," I said.

"You call what you do glamor? It ain't even living."

I finished my coffee, wished Thump good luck, and went out to the practice green to see if I could get a feel for dad's putter. It was probably foolish of me to decide that a tournament was a good place to try strange clubs for the first time. But it was a thing I wanted to do. I felt a little closer to my old man that way, maybe a little closer than I had felt when he was alive. I tried not to think that was it. I just felt a little warmer having the old man's clubs around, that's all.

He gave them to me a few months before he died. He was in his wheel chair and I was sitting on the couch. We weren't talking about anything in particular, and he said without emotion, "Do you want my clubs?" Without waiting for a response, he added, "Why don't you take them with you." When I had thought about this moment, which I knew someday would come, the scene had always been more dramatic, a sort of passing of the guard, the clubs embodying the wisdom of the game that dated clear back to the Royal and Ancient at St. Andrews.

But no. This was only the nearly final act of an invalid cleansing his life of accoutrements that had become no longer useful. It was also my father's only admission that he would never play golf again. And it passed between us without fanfare and without a trace.

When I put the clubs in my trunk, I ran my fingers over my father's name stitched on the side of the bag. It was not the name of some champion that all aspiring kids could look up to. It was the name of my father, a man without fame, but impossible to forget by anyone who ever knew him. He was who he was, whether it was good for him or not, and the endless roving that resulted from his dedication to maintaining that often tempestuous self was as much a requirement as a product.

His golf bag was a bright and tasteless yellow, his name in large green letters, certainly not anything I would have chosen to go with my otherwise pastel personality. At first, I thought, I certainly won't carry this bag where anyone can see me. But I did.

I did not touch the clubs until after my father died, and when I first took the clubs out to the practice range, I couldn't hit them. The grips were totally crooked, running every which way. My God, I thought, was the old man trying to compensate for his lack of power by forcing himself to grip the clubs in some arcane way? Did he think he had uncovered a bizarre secret to restoring his golf game?

My mother told me what happened. "A couple of years ago he got it into his head that he just had to regrip his clubs. He got the old ones off all right, but he just couldn't get the new ones on." I could see the old man, frailer by the day, battling an indifferent fate, the cork and rubber grips refusing to slide smoothly down the shafts. "I had to help him, but I wasn't strong enough either," my mother said. "We had all we could do to do two in an afternoon. We just got too tired." I could see them exhausted on either side of the living room—the old man no longer had a workbench—eyeing the golf clubs sprawled between them, the grips grinning crooked and defiant.

I regripped the clubs, even the putter.

Without thinking, I slapped a couple of practice putts. Mostly I was watching Harold Blaine tee off. He took one last drag through his hair with his comb and then rippled into the ball smooth as butter, and it whistled out over the first fairway, looking like it would never come down. Like most tall and thin guys, he hit it with a full arc, both feet flying, and made it work. His club connecting with the ball sounded like a rifle shot.

Blaine modeled himself on the Tour professionals in that he concentrated on golf the entire round. I doubt that he ever spoke to anybody once the round was under way. He watched this particular three-hundred-yard drive without changing the placid expression on his face. Just another day at the office. His team members, however, responded jubilantly, obviously pleased to have been paired with such a luminary.

Harold Blaine was new to the section the year Thump beat him for the Assistant Pro Championship. If I had known him better, I would have enjoyed the victory more. They had come to the last hole tied. Blaine had it fifteen feet from the cup in regulation. Thump was just barely on the green, about sixty feet, a slight hogback. Thump stood behind the putt a long time, holding his putter across his thighs, one hand on the grip, the other cupping the blade. Then he walked up and, without a practice stroke, knocked it into the hole. No ifs, no buts, the ball had "made" on it all the way.

Blaine turned white and reached for his long red comb. Even though he combed his hair the whole time he was looking over the putt, his ball never threatened the cup. For a long time after that he was wary of Thump, until it became clear that Thump had more important things on his mind than being a local tournament star, and his appearances at events became fewer and fewer.

My old man once beat Harold Blaine, and Blaine was not at all a sport about it. Blaine probably won ten pro-ams a year, and my old man probably won once in ten years. And Blaine couldn't believe it. "How could that fat old man shoot a score so low?" he went around asking. My old man just laughed. "I don't think Harold will ever congratulate me," he said. "Maybe I should buy him a new comb and try to make it up with him."

I got off the tee well enough with the old man's driver, and in fact I hit the ball squarely all day. I managed a couple of birdies, and with just two holes to play I was only a couple over par. I began to think about the possibility of getting paid. That would be a sort of sentimental tribute to the old man's clubs, I thought. At one of the drinking fountains I met Sonny, who was a few holes behind me. His collar was up the way the good players of his day wore it, his hair was awry, and the color was drained from his face.

"You in a death struggle with the course?" I asked.

"I'm even par," he announced, an exaggerated southern drawl on the last word. Harold Blaine wasn't the only guy who could pretend he was on Tour.

"Go get 'em," I said and gave up any thought of finishing in the money myself. If Sonny was matching the card, guys like Harold Blaine and Thump must be walking the ball around in practically nothing. I decided to get it into the clubhouse as best I could and try to keep from embarrassing myself. As it turned out, Sonny didn't stay at par, but he didn't play badly.

Through the combination of some guys playing a little less impressively than normal, and my scoring lower than usual, I qualified tenth. I couldn't believe it. Not only was I going to make a decent check in the tournament, I was in the derby. In a derby, the ten low pros play nine holes, the high score dropping out on each hole. In case of a tie, there is a pitch-off from about ten yards. The player farthest from the hole is out. We call them derbies because people buy parimutuel tickets on the players as in a horse race.

I went into the locker room to wash my face. Sonny was there changing clothes. "Hey," he said. "You're playing." Without waiting for a response, he forged on in the inimitable O'Brien fashion. "I came close to the derby. Missed by two.

Closest I've ever come. Blaine was low, you see? Thump had a good round, huh?" He stood up from tying his shoes and buckled his belt, red on bright-yellow doubleknits.

"Anyway, you finished in the money, Sonny," I said, toweling the soap out of my ears.

"Yeah, oh yeah. You play hard out there now. I'm betting on ya. Already bought a ticket."

"Okay, Sonny," I said as he strode out. Quite a Sonny. He knew how to have a good time. He would spend far more celebrating his tie for twelfth than his prize would pay for. And he would strut all night.

My strategy was simple. Don't choke. I tried to hit the ball square and get my hands through the ball, and even though I had to pitch off a couple of times, I avoided disaster. On the 8th tee, it was Thump, Harold Blaine, and me. I nearly took the skin off my hands trying to get rid of the sweat. Harold looked at me sideways as if he wanted to say, "What the devil are you doing here?" I gave him my own snide sideways look. "I think I'll get me a comb so I can play the last two holes," I said. Thump walked over and gave me a pat in the rump with the head of his driver.

We all parred. In the pitch-off, Thump caught his wedge a bit clean and the ball rolled too far. Harold and I walked to the 9th tee. The hole was a 3-par, about a full 9-iron to an elevated green. Harold caught his a little on the inside and pulled it twenty feet left of the hole. Still he was safely on. Since I saw he had hit a 9 and I was generally a club or two behind the good players, I thought I'd better hit an 8. I hadn't counted on my own adrenaline, and the ball landed too deep into the green and rolled over the back, down the bank, and into thick rough.

When Harold saw my lie from atop the green bank, he smirked and put his comb away. But he shouldn't have. The rough had been walked down, and even though the grass was long, it lay mostly flat. There was no air between the ball and the ground. I took out the sand wedge, opened my stance, and put the wrists to it. The ball took off like a shot, just clearing the bank. "That's gone for good," Harold said in his lazy melody of a voice. I ran up the bank to watch. In midair, the ball died three feet short of the flagstick, thumped onto the green, squiggled a bit, and rolled into the cup. Harold took his comb out.

But missed his putt. Later in the clubhouse, I heard him tell somebody, "Dumb luck. What can you do? That sort of thing always happens when you're playing some hacker. What a fluke. One lousy shot." Harold was at a back corner table and I was at the bar, drinking with Sonny.

"You know, Sonny," I said, "a nice guy would say that I had played at the top of my game for once in my life, and it was just his bad luck to have been in my way."

Sonny snorted into his glass. The whiskey and water made bubbles of sorts. "Harold Blaine is not a nice guy," he said.

I wondered what the old man would do. I decided to do

a little hot-dogging of my own. "Harold," I shouted. I didn't turn to face him, but just addressed his reflection in the mirror behind the bar. The noise dropped and everybody seemed to be looking at me. "I couldn't help it," I shouted, even louder once I had his attention. "I was playing with my old man's clubs. He must have left me a few good shots."

6

Everybody Wins

"You drive all night to get here?" the old man asked. He was covering his eggs with pepper.

"Naw. I left the Cities at two this morning," I said. "I decided I wanted to be unconscious while I was around here." I chased the marmalade to the four corners of my toast.

"Well, I'm going to play damn well today," the old man said. There was a bitter twist to his voice.

"Now, don't let that bother you," my mother said. Her jaw was set firmly, and she had her hand on the old man's shoulder.

We were sitting in the dining room of the country club where my mother had been club champion. In the downstairs bar there was a copper plaque that listed all the women's club champions. There was no name for the year my mother won. Just a blank space.

For ten years the old man had been skipping this pro-am, but this year my parents were working a club that was just an hour away, and my mother wanted him to play so she could see old friends. For me, the tournament was a five-hour drive, and I don't as a rule stray that far from home. I hadn't been playing well enough to enter any tournaments, but my mother thought it would be fun if we were all there, so I agreed to meet them and caddie for the old man.

"I'm going to go out and take their golf course apart and feed it to 'em chunk by chunk." The old man was wolfing his eggs.

"You're not going to play well if you stay worked up," my mother said in her cautious voice.

"Oh, all right," the old man said, in that grumpy way he had whenever she almost scolded him.

The old man went out to chip and putt, and I ducked into the locker room. Harold Blaine was in front of the mirror, sculpting his wave, his long red comb just barely touching his hair. I pushed by him without saying anything.

"Hey, I didn't know you were coming down here," he said in a forced jovial tone. "We could have rode together." He squinted and tilted his head back and forth to check his wave from all directions.

"I just got here this morning," I said, tending to my business.

"You bring your uncle Thump with you?" Blaine asked, pausing with his comb and turning halfway toward me.

"Thump doesn't play much these days," I said. "He mostly just likes to stay around home and watch his two little girls grow up."

Blaine went back to combing his hair. I like to think he was actually worried that Thump might have entered. "I came down yesterday," he said. "I wanted a practice round. I've been low pro here three times."

"You could say that about every tournament in the section," I said, moving to the sink.

Blaine snorted approval and smiled big.

"We tee off on number 10, Mr. Blaine," a deep and phlegmy voice said behind us.

I looked up from my soapy hands. "How are you, Mr. Rasmussen?" I said to his reflection.

Mike Rasmussen had more gray hair than I remembered, and his shoulders had sagged considerably. But I could still see that he'd been a strong man in his time. He waited until I had dried my hands before taking my right one in both of his. "It's sure been a while since we've seen your face around here." He seemed pleased to see me.

"You on Harold's team?" I said. Blaine had gone on to the course.

"That I am," Mike said. His huge smile seemed to bring his shoulders to attention.

"You'll see some good golf," I said. "And how is Mrs. Rasmussen?"

"Just fine," he said, finally letting go of my hand. "She'll be tickled to know you're here. She always said if we'd had any kids, she's have wanted a son like you."

I smiled. Mike turned and hurried after Blaine, and I stopped to check myself in the mirror. There on the toiletry shelf was Blaine's comb. A couple of hairs waved at me from the teeth.

When we worked this club and I was my old man's assistant, Mike Rasmussen was one of our good customers. He had been a big-deal football star at the state ag college, and he liked to think of himself as a championship player although I don't ever remember him breaking 80. He was some kind of salesman, and he had the salesman's knack for telling jokes and laughing. He was a sweet guy and I liked him.

He would get in off the road early on Fridays sometimes and he and Monica Rasmussen would come out and shoot nine before having dinner at the club. Since Friday was a slow day, I could usually get out of the shop to play. Lots of times I played with them. Because I could sneak the score in under 40, he thought I was a hell of a player, or he liked to make me think he did.

He was forever wanting to know what kind of balls I played with, or what clubs I was now using. After the round he would come in the shop and buy a dozen balls and then make the old man an offer he couldn't refuse for my clubs. I didn't complain. I knew Mike was giving us more than they were worth. And his game wouldn't improve, and we'd go through it all again in a week or two and I'd get back whatever set I was fond of, for a while.

I liked Mike, but I was in love with Monica. She was in her early forties, and she had brown eyes that I felt in the pit of my stomach. Every muscle she owned was perfect. Her body was without flab, except at key points. Since I was in my late teens, erotic fantasies were my favorite hobby, and dreaming about Monica Rasmussen was my particular pastime.

Mike really didn't have time to tend his acreage, and since I worked around golf courses, he figured I knew something about lawns; so he paid me twenty-five dollars to come out once a week to ride around on his tractor mower. Every third or fourth time, I would have to trim his hedges with an electric clipper. That's all I had to do.

The old man wasn't crazy about having me gone from the shop one morning a week, but I argued it would be good for member rapport. The old man laughed and shook his head. "I don't know how we could get him to spend any more money," he said.

After my work was done Monica always had me come into the house for a glass of tea. It was a large house, and she took care of it all by herself. Everything was tasteful. Hardwood floors, expensive rugs. Art objects all around on little platforms. Lots of open space. When I drank my tea, Monica would sit at the dining room table and talk to me.

You can imagine what happened. I could imagine it, and in fact, did so daily, but I couldn't believe it.

It wasn't as if we had some kind of torrid heavy-breathing rip-your-clothes-off sort of thing. Something happened only three times. And it happened only once, really. I never knew what was going to happen when I went to cut the grass. Nothing was ever prearranged. I only hoped that she would be there and that she would talk to me.

I never knew what to say, and she would ask me about myself. Then after a couple of such conversations, she asked, "You aren't very good at this, are you?" I looked confused. "Ask me about myself. Women like to talk about themselves." So I asked her why she didn't play in the important club tournaments for women.

There I found the only reason I ever had to be frustrated with Mike. Monica was one of the best women players at the club. The first year they were members, she was women's club champion. That was the only year she had entered the tournament. "Good wives should not do things that will outshine their husbands," she said, and I guess she believed herself. The only tournaments she entered were husband-and-wife events, which they very often won, thanks to her playing.

Monica's and my first time, I was sitting in a chair and Monica was standing behind me, having just poured my tea.

She set the pitcher down and rested her strong golfer's forearms on my shoulders. She bent down and began to nibble my ears. Her silky blondish-brown hair fell over my face. I froze. I wasn't going to object, but I didn't know what to do. "You're awfully sweaty," she said. "You'd better take a shower." That's what I meant about this not being one of those out-of-control sort of things. I had to take a shower each time.

I caddied, and the old man shot 76, which in and of itself would have disappointed him on a course he knew so well, but it was twice as bad today because he felt like he had let Mother down. "Hey," I said. "This revenge business is your idea. Ma doesn't care. She knows who won that tournament."

"But I'm still mad," he said.

The old man was so busy being unhappy with himself that he failed to notice that the great Harold Blaine, defending pro medalist, had made 78 and was sulking in the locker room, refusing to talk to anybody. In fact, he squealed his Texas Cadillac out of the parking lot before the awards dinner.

The Rasmussens sat with us at the dinner. Monica was still beautiful. There were streaks of gray in her hair, and her skin was still taut. Her voice was soft. Although she spent most of the time talking with my mother, Monica was very warm toward me. She was very interested in what I had been doing, and seemed a little disappointed that I was not yet a head pro.

"It takes a long time to get a head job at the kind of clubs I work," I said. "I don't have enough wrinkles yet." I hoped she wouldn't think I was being haughty. "Those people with old money like to have old pros."

Monica laughed and reached across the table to take my hand in hers. Her wedding ring looked particularly gold against her suntanned fingers. "You'll be old soon enough," she said. "And you'll be kinder."

"I thought we had a sure thing with this Blaine guy," Mike said. He was wiggling a piece of roast beef around on his fork. "You should have seen the drive he hit on number 10. Damn near 300 yards."

"Big hitter," I said.

"Then," Mike raised his voice, "halfway down the fairway, he reaches for his comb and he can't find it."

"He combs his hair to calm his nerves," I said. "Always carries it in his back pocket."

"Well, there's no comb, and he bogeys four of the first seven holes and is about ready to check himself into the hospital. We're turning our bags inside out looking for anything that might resemble a comb."

"Couldn't he just buy one?" Monica asks.

"Not in the middle of a golf course," Mike says. "But I do know we spent a bundle for our team in the calcutta, and we ain't gonna see a nickel of that money again."

The old man was still so taken with being mad at himself that he failed to notice until it was announced that his team had taken second. The old man's team had gone for

$240. The teams had the option of buying half of themselves, and the old man had picked up his twelve-and-a-half percent. The calcutta paid $1,700 for second, so with the addition of his prize money and pari-mutuel tickets on his team, the old man had close to a $600 day, mostly in cash.

"We'll have to go down and set the house up," the old man said, not bothering to count the wad of bills that was unrolling itself beside his plate.

"Now, you don't have to go spending it just because you won it," my mother said, in her cautious voice. She didn't look at the old man, but she gave Monica and Mike a quiet smile.

"Oh, all right," he said, exasperated.

"We've told you about that time Daddy made a hole in one in a tournament," my mother said to me.

"Won a set of woods and irons," I said, toward the Rasmussens.

"Yes, by God," the old man said. "I only had one myself, but I bought everybody in the field a drink."

"Well, I don't know about everybody," my mother said. "But he had to auction off the woods to pay his bar bill." She laughed.

"When I win, everybody wins," the old man said. "Most of the people I've played golf with in my life don't even know how to have a good time."

"Well, by God, you can buy me a drink," Mike said.

With Mike on his arm, the old man strode triumphantly into the bar, brandishing a fist of bills, ready to set up the house. Mother marched right after him. Every time he bought somebody a drink, she beat him to the change, and every time he set the roll down, she sidearmed a few bills off the top.

"I think Ma's got her Danish up," I said.

"I think so, too," the old man said. "And she'll get most of it home."

A few years ago my mother told me that an anonymous club member had paid to have her name engraved on the champions' plaque. No one would tell her who it was.

"Must have been Mike Rasmussen," I said.

"Or Monica," my mother said.

7

As Important As Life Itself

My father's decision to become a golf professional was his own drama played out without fanfare. Few besides my mother understood the intensity in the blood that drew him toward golf. He came up in the game in the thirties: caddie, caddie-master, assistant pro. Then he was sidetracked by World War II, then by fatherhood. When he got back from the war, he found being a fireman was the perfect job for someone who wanted to develop as a golfer. You work every other day. On his days off he went to the practice tee and built his golf swing. And he made himself a good player.

His golf was played mostly at the old home club. The nine-hole course was one of the earliest built in the state of Minnesota. It was short by contemporary standards, measuring only 3,000 yards, but it was tight, hilly, and wooded. The sand traps were deep, the rough dense, and the greens elevated and small. You had to know how to turn the ball in all directions, hit it high and low, usually from side-hill and uphill lies.

My father entered a few local amateur tournaments, but only one had any meaning for him. The shortstop played at the hometown club over Labor Day. In the late forties and early fifties, it drew one of the fastest fields of any of the minor tournaments around the state. Numerous state amateur champions and other hotshots from the Twin Cities competed regularly, and many failed to qualify for the championship flight which was limited to the low sixteen scores. These sixteen played rounds of match play on Sunday and Labor Day, and ultimately the finals between the two remaining undefeated were held Labor Day afternoon. Tournaments like these were called "shortstops" because once you were defeated, you were through, you were "shortstopped."

For my father the shortstop represented initiation into the profession. Wally Ulrich had won it in 1946 and gone on to a career on the PGA Tour. Ulrich putted for a 59 in the second round of the Virginia Beach Classic in 1953. He left the thirty-footer ten inches short, dead on line with the jar.

In 1954, he won the Kansas City Open by two shots over Gene Littler. Ulrich's last-round 66 included a 31 on the front nine.

Ulrich, who lived in a town thirty miles from the old hometown, had been the old man's friend since they were kids. Ulrich would stop by a couple times every summer, and he and the old man would play. Wally's bulbish nose sunburned easily, and I don't know that I ever saw him outside without that nose covered in thick white cream. That Ulrich had a high opinion of my father's golf game did not exactly help the old man settle into a life as small-town fireman and local good player. He couldn't get it out of his head that Wally Ulrich, PGA Tour pro, told him more than once, "You can play. You ought to give it a try."

"I'm going to win the shortstop and turn pro," became the litany riding on the tune of his golf swing. But the old man put too much pressure on himself. Although he always qualified in the low sixteen, he made it past the first round only once. In 1951, he reached the finals and lost the tournament on the last hole. He was against one of the Twin Cities hot dogs, an older competitor who had already won the tournament four times. Two down at the turn, my father managed to square things by the 18th tee. But on the final hole, he drove right of the trees bordering the fairway. Rather than punch the ball back into play, he tried to shove it through a space he thought he saw in the branches between himself and the green. The opening wasn't there.

He was thirty-one years old. That night just before he

went to bed, he looked at my mother across the living room and said, "I can't wait any longer. Tomorrow, I'm a pro."

Back in the fifties the PGA Tour was not the megabucks proposition that it is now. You had to be a PGA member to play, and to be a PGA member you had to come up through the ranks. You had to have served as an assistant or head pro at a golf course for five years. On tour, you had to consistently finish in the top ten to even hope of earning a living. Pros shared car rides between tournaments and crowded into cheap motels. Their biggest hopes were that a few good years on tour would land them lucrative club jobs. Many of the big-name players were actually club pros who spent much of the year in their pro shops and on the lesson tee.

The old man kept his job with the fire department, but he served as pro at the hometown club, giving lessons and running club events. He also went around to smaller clubs in the area and gave lessons.

Uncle Thump's amateur career was more widely ranging and therefore more famous than my father's. Being a natural, he matured early and won the state high school championship two times. He was second in the national junior and low amateur in the St. Paul Open. All this before he was nineteen. He was a raw-boned, skinny kid with big ears and a perfect golf swing. If he had a flaw, it seemed to be that he did not have a strong winner-take-all instinct. He won tournaments because he shot the lowest scores, not because he set out to pin everybody's ears back.

There was some talk in the old hometown about

putting Thump on the Tour, but in the old hometown there is always more talk than money. The high rollers at the country club usually only roll their tongues.

Thump and the old man shared the course record on the old hometown course, 30, 6 under par. I have a stark memory from when I was very young, maybe only two or three. My father has just finished his round. He seems not to acknowledge my mother and me, who for some unrecalled reason have come to the course, a rare thing for us to do, to meet him. He walks off the final green, breaks a club by wrapping it around a small tree, and throws his golf ball across two fairways and into a third.

He had needed only par on the final hole to shoot 28; even a bogey would have given him a new course record. The 9th hole was 350 yards long, but there was nothing between the tee and the severely elevated green but two ridges. You wanted to hit your drive to the center of the second ridge. The fairway fell away on both sides. On the right was a line of trees that you couldn't hit over if you strayed off the fairway. Deep sand traps sat at each of the front corners of the green. Behind the green was air; if you went over, you had it fifty yards back out of the 1st fairway.

The old man had plopped his second shot into one of the traps. Normally a good sand player, he was too anxious this time and, looking up, bladed the shot over the green. His temper took control from there, and he limped out of the hole with an 8.

The club he wrapped around a tree was the Wilson R20, the first real sand wedge, which Gene Sarazen developed in the early thirties. In the way golfers have, my father lamented the loss of that particular club for the rest of his life. Even exact copies never felt as good, nor ever worked as well.

The hometown crowd never quite grasped the importance my father invested in professional golf. They seemed not to take him seriously. If he wanted to give lessons and pick up some extra money, that was all right with them. But surely he knew he was not as good a player as Wally Ulrich. In fact, they were not at all sure he could beat his kid brother, Thump, who still in his teens was winning every amateur tournament in southern Minnesota and northern Iowa.

At the end of every summer, it seemed, my father was having to explain to someone or other that he couldn't enter the shortstop. "It's an amateur tournament," he would say with less and less patience. "I'm a pro." Perhaps they were asking because they knew how much winning it would mean to him, or maybe they just couldn't bring themselves to take his aspirations seriously, or maybe they didn't want him to take himself too seriously. But when he would explain that he was earning his PGA card, they would say things like, "I'm sure no one would mind if you played, would they?" and he would quickly make them uncomfortable with retorts like, "I would. I would mind very much."

Perhaps to accentuate his new status, my father always

entered the St. Paul Open. For one week a summer, he was a touring pro. Not only did he go to St. Paul, but he also went to Waterloo. The city of Waterloo, Iowa, held the Waterloo Open on the Sunday of the St. Paul Open. First prize was a thousand dollars.

Even though the money trailed off sharply after that, almost all the touring pros who missed the cut in St. Paul drove to Waterloo and played thirty-six holes on Sunday. My father went with them because he never made the cut at the St. Paul Open, and during those years he never figured seriously at Waterloo, although twice he made a hundred dollars in the driving contest, once for most accurate and once for longest drive. His normal drive was 260 to 275 yards, impressive distances for the equipment and balls of the late forties and early fifties.

The year he won for long drive, he thrilled the crowd with a trick he had seen Babe Didrikson employ during her exhibition play. His first ball went into the rough, which took him out of contention for the accuracy prize. His second attempt stopped rolling at 277. After teeing up his third and last ball, he walked to the back of the tee to confer with the official. A two-way radio conversation confirmed that 277 was 5 yards short of first place. He sighted down the fairway, strode toward his ball, and swung on the run, the follow-through carrying him off the front of the tee. 303 yards. No contest.

My old man couldn't play like Wally Ulrich, and he certainly hadn't distinguished himself like Thump, but one thing he could do well was play for his own money. He would play anybody, anywhere, for money he couldn't afford to lose, and he could play like gangbusters. He never hustled pigeons, but he didn't turn them down. "You make the game. I'll play it," was his usual reply.

One day a bunch of the locals whose pockets he'd been picking came up with a proposition. Since he thought he was such a hot player, they had gone to the trouble of finding somebody they figured he couldn't beat. Somebody from out of town, somebody he didn't know. They were willing to back this mystery player to an eighteen-hole match, a hundred-dollar nassau, if the old man wanted any of that action.

"On my own golf course?" the old man asked, incredulous. "Right here?"

"Right here."

The old man just shook his head. "You guys can't be serious. I'd play Ben Hogan for money on my own golf course."

The match was arranged, but no name was mentioned. Meanwhile, they had gone to Thump and told him they were going to back him in a match with a fellow who needed to be put in his place. Again they mentioned no name.

It was a Sunday morning. My old man was waiting on the tee. The gamblers slowly began to show up, but there was no mystery player. The old man was beginning to wonder if this guy would be small or big, if he hit it long or short, and if he would recognize the name.

He noticed Thump's car pulling into the parking lot.

"Maybe I'll see if the kid brother wants to caddie for me," he said. There was a little uneasiness among the crowd. Thump got out of the car, took his clubs from the trunk, and began to change into his golf shoes.

My father still didn't catch on. "I don't see any of his buddies around. He must be going to practice. I'll talk him out of that."

Thump walked up to the first tee, greeting everyone in his usual unassuming way. Then he looked at his older brother. "You gonna play with us?" he asked. "They got some good player they want to match me against."

My dad's shoulders fell three inches, and he stared at the crowd with a look that was somewhere between hurt and bewilderment. There was an attempt at raucous laughter, but it fell quickly to nervous laughter, and then there was silence. The old man continued to stare and never did look Thump in the eye.

"This is who you want me to play?" Thump asked at last.

One of the crowd said, "We just wanted to see what you'd do."

"We wanted to see who was best," another one said.

Thump and the old man never looked at each other. Thump looked at the crowd, and my father didn't look at much of anything. He just sort of stared off into the distance like he was waiting for the whole thing to be over, like he was trapped in somebody else's bad dream.

After everybody had as much silence as they could handle, Thump spoke. "I ain't playing him."

Thump walked off the tee, got into his car without changing his spikes, and drove home.

Thump was out in my grandfather's front yard, hitting practice balls over the football field into the lake. He wasn't thinking about his swing or how the balls were traveling. He was hitting one after another. His mouth was turned down.

My father parked across the street and walked slowly up the dusty drive and over to watch Thump. Thump kept hitting. "Lord, what natural action you've got," the old man said after a while. "Don't ever lose that."

"I don't care," Thump said, his cheeks turning red.

"Well, give it to me then, boy," the old man said in a loud, humorous way. "I could use it."

"Don't those guys know I wouldn't even play this game if it weren't for my brother?" Thump said. "What's wrong with 'em anyway? It's like they can't leave nothing alone."

"Pay no attention to those idiots," the old man said. "I'll get 'em back. I'll get so deep into their pockets they won't know what hit 'em."

Thump teed up a ball and handed the old man his driver. "Hit this one," he said.

The old man swung the club and the ball moved high and long, dropping to a slight fade before disappearing into the lake.

8

Listening to the Game

The summer after my father died, I started teaching at one of the old-money country clubs in St. Paul. The course is tight and hilly. You have to work the ball, constantly playing for position. There aren't a lot of trees, but if you stray from the fairway, the trees seem to be miraculously in the way. I make a good living teaching mediocre players how to have more fun at golf by hitting the ball straight.

I met Geegee on a Saturday night. She was twenty or twenty-one. I was forty-two. She sought me out because of my father. There was some sort of formal-gown gathering up in the dining room, and I was down in the back shop, catching up on club repairs.

Geegee came into the back shop in a lavender gown that showed off the deep tan of her shoulders. Her black hair was in tight curls that ended at the neck, and her eyes were chestnut brown. I was in the middle of regripping a 5-iron. Since this country club was the sort you didn't get into until you'd earned your tenth or eleventh million, I figured she was some member's granddaughter who had the good sense to be bored at this particular festive occasion and had gone exploring.

"You're likely to get dirty in here, miss," I said, sliding the grip on, and moving quickly to set the club down and line up the Vs on the grip with the clubface. "We usually don't let the members come back here."

"I want to play the Tour," she said.

"You could really get seriously dirty back here," I said.

"I want a lesson," she said. "The word is old Al has gone and hired himself a pro who can really teach. You play in tournaments much?"

"Not often," I said, reaching for another iron to regrip.

"I didn't think so," she said, looking directly at me and paying no attention to my workbench or my chores. I was kind of hurt by that. I never have gotten over the pride I had as a young man at being a clubsmith, at knowing the little secrets about how golf clubs are put together and how they work.

"I had never heard of you," she continued. "So I thought maybe you could teach. I've had a lot of lessons from guys who want to play tournaments."

"You're smart," I said, warming to her for the first time.

I picked up a driver I had reshafted the week before and set about completing the whipping. I held the wooden clubhead up where she could see it. "This clubhead must be thirty years old," I said.

She glanced at it without focusing. It was the only time she wasn't drilling into me with her chestnut eyes. "I play metal," she said.

"Metal hits it farther," I said.

"I'll be out Monday," she said.

"Monday's full," I said.

"I don't want a lesson," she said. "Not yet. I just want to watch. I want to see if you know your stuff, or if you're just a golf bum."

I let the golf bum comment pass. I figured people like her in her lavender gown at this club where they keep their money in mothballs probably shouldn't even try to understand people like me.

"I'll be expecting you, then."

She held out her hand, and for the first time in our conversation, smiled. "I'm Geegee."

I recognized the name. The week before she had

finished somewhere among the leaders in the State Women's Amateur Stroke-Play Championship. I rummaged through a stack of newspapers back in my room and found the results. Geegee was fifth. A second-round 71 had left her in danger of winning, and women amateurs being as they are, that one low score had been enough to keep her four-round total near the top. There were really only a dozen or so good women players in the state, and Geegee obviously was one of them.

When I asked Al about her, he frowned. "That little brat pesters the hell out of every teaching assistant I bring in here. Don't let her tie you up on the range. You just run her little butt out of there."

"Appears to be a good player," I said.

"Oh, she can play," he said. "But you just run her off. She'll come down here and whine. I've been whining back at her for over ten years."

I liked Al. He was over sixty, about ready to retire. Even stooped by age, he still stood over six feet. He had huge hands that must have been eight inches across the back. You notice that about good players. They almost always have these big, powerful hands. Al was still strong. His swing barely covered the distance from hip to hip, and he could still hit the driver 250. "I've really shortened up," he'd say.

He'd been a player up in the Northeast in his youth, and had taken a turn or two at the Tour. At some point he'd lost the Metropolitan PGA to some hot dog off the Tour. He loved to tell about it. "I'm in the clubhouse, and I really figure I've got it in my pocket. Last hole's a par 4. 420. Big hole.

Creek ten, fifteen feet wide runs in front of the green. Picturesque damn creek, full of rocks, goldfish, crap like that. You don't catch the driver just right, you have to think twice about going for the green.

"Well, the only guy on the course that can beat me hits a good drive. But I'm still not worried. But I should have been. I just figured this was my time. I mean, I thought the championship was in my pocket.

"So this guy from the Tour pulls out a 5-iron. And skulls it. I see the ball scraping along the ground, and I can't believe he choked. But the ball just keeps skipping and hopping. Right along into the creek. Hits a rock—and this is no lie—bounces off a turtle. Yes, honest to God, a turtle's back. Big old mud turtle. Mean and ugly. Opens his mouth like he's complaining about being hit, and I'm struck by how pink his mouth is. I mean, I'm in the process of losing the Met PGA and I'm struck by how pink a turtle's mouth is. Well, that ball skips right up onto the green and rolls into the hole.

"Hell, I didn't even have a chance to beat the son-of-a-bitch in a play-off. For months after that I'd close my eyes at night trying to get to sleep and all I could see was that turtle's pink mouth."

Geegee showed up at the range when I was halfway through my first lesson. Since the members of this club don't work, a normal day begins at nine, or later. She took a spot under a tree close enough to see what was going on. I was afraid she would make my lessons nervous, but nobody really seemed to notice her. A few said hello on arriving or leaving. Geegee's watching lessons seemed quite normal to them. I stayed on the tee until five, without lunch. Geegee neither spoke to me nor strayed from the shade the whole time.

Remembering what Al said, I thought I should just head for the pro shop when I was done, but instead I went over to the tree and sat beside her. "Well, you saw all manner of swings today," I said. "I don't know why golf attracts so many ill-coordinated people."

"Golf is still a country-club sport for these folks," she said without inflection. "They play to maintain what they think is their place in the social order."

"Lucky for me, they do," I said.

"You're not a player, are you?" she said.

"What makes you say that?"

"Most pros take Monday off. There's usually a pro-am or a jackpot tournament around somewhere." She was right. The old man had won a jackpot tournament once. Went 68-70 in a drizzle and made 150 bucks.

"I give lessons when people want them," I said. "I play a little in September and October before heading south or west. Wherever I can line something up for the winter."

She seemed not to pay attention to what I was saying. "And when you demonstrate the importance of the left hand, you put the ball on a tee and hit it one-handed with a 7-iron."

"So?"

"Your father hits it off the ground one-handed with a 5-iron."

Geegee had not had a lesson from the old man, but when she was a junior-higher she had seen him demonstrate at the PGA golf camp, something he did the last few years before he got really bad. "I didn't think I was good enough then to ask him to help me," she said. "But the older kids all said your father was the one to work with if you were a good player. He could make you better."

I handed her my 7-iron. "Hit a couple," I said.

"Not yet," she said. "I haven't made my mind up yet. All I saw you do today was stuff anyone could have gotten out of Tommy Armour's book."

My pride was hurt. I remembered that I was talking to a snot-nosed country-club brat who evidently could play a bit and thought that made her somehow important. "These folks needed fundamentals. And besides, even if they read the books, they wouldn't understand 'em. They need somebody to make 'em do it. They need to have the hands laid on, so to speak."

"Hit a nerve, did I?" she asked. She smirked. Her mouth turned up at the corners, creating a little dent in her upper lip, and her eyes dared me to speak.

With a golf club, Geegee was picture-book stylish. She swooped down at the ball from a full turn and finished with her hands high. When it worked, she hit high floaters that landed and rolled without so much as a dimple. When it didn't work, she lost a lot of shots to the right.

"You look nice," I said. "But you're not hitting the ball

with anything. I'm surprised you score as well as you do." I took her up to the range and crouched down behind her. With both hands, I held her left heel to the ground. "Hit until I tell you to stop."

She didn't have to hit more than a half-dozen. "Do you feel yourself hitting the ball?" She frowned. "Do you feel the power in your hands?" She wouldn't have admitted it even if she had. "You can't get by with that cute little rocking swoop now. You have to make your hands work."

She looked at me in the way that I best remember her. Her head tilts right, the tip of her tongue rests outside the corner of her mouth, and her brown eyes are at once here and far away like her brain is slowly processing what you are saying to her. "You work on keeping your left heel down," I said.

I thought that would be the last of her, but the next week she came to the range every morning and hit two or three buckets of balls. She worked through her bag systematically, hitting every shot with her heel down, and assessing the results. The ball seemed to move with more authority. I kept a half an eye on her from my lessons, but I didn't speak to her. And she chose not to speak to me.

The next Monday morning she was back hitting balls. She left around noon, and again we didn't speak. That evening just as I sent my last lesson on his way, she showed up. "Let's play," she said. "We can get in three or four holes before dark."

"I don't need to play," I said, holding my 5-iron behind by back, "but I'll walk along with you. Or, if you want, we could take a cart and get in more than three or four holes."

She rolled her eyes and her mouth tilted into a sneer. "In the first place, I don't use carts. I walk. I need to feel the course underneath me. Carts are not golf. I have to breathe on the course. I have to sense what's going to happen to the ball."

I didn't know what to say to that. I had not thought breathing on the course was any different than breathing anywhere else.

"And in the second place," she added, "you play."

So I played. And that became our routine. She would hit balls all morning and come back to the range in early evening, and we would bat out a few holes before dark. It never occurred to me to wonder how she knew when I would be done, until one day Al asked, "What is that young woman doing looking in your lesson book all the time?" Al didn't hang around much once all the late players were on the course, so he didn't know Geegee and I were playing a few holes each evening. "Oh, I'm doing a little work on her game," I said.

"She'll waste your time," he said.

"My old man used to work with her at golf camp," I said. "You know, when she was just a kid."

"Really?" Al said, his lower lip sticking out and his forehead forming into wrinkles. "Hmmm." If my old man had worked with her, maybe my showing her game attention might make some sense. The world is full of good players that nobody likes, but a good player is a good player.

I'd been conscious of my attraction to Geegee, but I didn't think I would ever act on anything. But once we got caught by darkness a couple of holes from the clubhouse.

"We tried to play too many holes," I said. "I had a feeling we were biting off more than we could chew."

"I don't mind," she said. "It's rather pleasant out here. The night is cooling things off."

"We can pretend we're out for a walk," I said, taking her hand, something I had never done. In fact, I had put my hands on her only in the course of golf instruction.

She squeezed my hand and stepped in front of me, presenting her face, quizzical and white in the dark. After a kiss that was mostly her teeth, I said in a way that wanted to be taken seriously, but was comic enough to save face, "I think I love you." And she said, "I love you, too," in a sort of croaking way as if she wasn't used to saying it. Almost immediately, she covered what I took to be true emotion by laughing. "You are really corny, you know that," she said, but she did not move away from my embrace.

"I always figure honesty works best," I said.

Then she said, "Come home with me." Just like that. It was the first time I knew she had her own place.

I gave Geegee the golf swing that made her a winner, that took her out of the elite ladies' championships and put her on the Tour. She probably wouldn't credit me if you asked her, but she should. All you have to do is watch her play.

"Look," I said, after we were close enough for me to talk sternly to her. "Take that stylish follow-through some idiot gave you and throw it in the ash can. All I want you to think about is throwing your boobs down the fairway after you hit the ball. Make your hands hit the living shit out of it and get the club as far through the ball as you can. And when you're done, don't worry if you've wrapped the club around your neck."

She glared at me and pulled a range ball into her stance.

"And another thing," I said. "You can let your left heel come up a bit now."

Well, she tried it, and it wasn't long before it was working. "You're not so calculated and dainty, anymore," I said one day on the range. "You're hitting it with heart, desire, spirit, whatever you want to call it."

I also made Geegee a real putter. She couldn't make anything over six feet, and was lucky to get a twenty- or thirty-footer anywhere near the hole. All I did was move the ball back in her stance so she would accelerate through the ball. She began to putt the eyes out of 'em. She won four women's invitationals and took second in the State Match-Play Championship.

I never went to the tournaments to watch her play. Almost every weekday, she hit balls and played, and, when I was done with lessons, we would play a few holes in the evenings. Three or four days a week she would ask me to come home with her.

Sometimes we would get a video movie, and she would cook for me. But we never appeared in public off the golf course. Nobody, I'm sure, thought our golf dates were strange because Geegee was very open about how I was helping her with her game. She even thanked me over television when she was runner-up in the State Match Play.

I was her golf pro, pure and simple. I never met her family. Her grandparents were club members, but they never came near me. She never introduced us.

I play a little more golf now than I did for many years before I knew Geegee. I got so I didn't mind playing if I was playing with her because she enjoyed it so much. She positively gurgled on every shot. Her eyes applauded the game itself. Golf was mostly what we talked about, her golf, her game, her future.

My theory was that Minnesota was a tough place to get launched from. She needed to be in the South where she could play all year, where she could come to the attention of people with money. She laughed, her mouth turning up at the corners. Her grandparents had enough money. I had forgotten who I was talking to. And so it was. She didn't need a manager. Right now, she needed a teacher, and I was it.

"I've always wanted to do it in a sand trap." Geegee curled into the crook of my arm. I buried my face deep into her curls. Her scalp smelled clean. It was three in the morning, a light rain was falling, and we were in the sand trap on the 7th hole. It was a deep trap left of the green and had caught many pulled approaches.

Our sexual energies exhausted for what I hoped would be only the moment, we were languishing deep in the soft sand. She had made me rake our portion of the trap when we decided to come down into it. "They will see our butt prints in the sand in the morning," she said.

I smiled at the thought. It would be the morning the women had the course exclusively. I wondered what they would make of the clear form of my hind end and Geegee's hip in the sand. "Will you be playing? You could interpret the findings for them."

She snuggled closer and sighed a long sigh. "We may still be asleep here when they show up."

I became chilled at the thought of all the women in the club ringing the trap pointing at us. Most would be aghast. Some of the more liberal would be bemused. "Well, that would certainly settle the question of how much longer I will be hanging around here," I said.

"What do you mean, how much longer?" Geegee asked. "Most of these randy old ladies out here are so hard up, once they find out you put out, you'll probably triple your lessons. Besides, you're not going anywhere. You're going to take over from Al. You're going to be head pro."

I began to kiss her neck. "We already did that," she said. "I want to talk about this head-pro thing."

I moved my cheek along the line of her chin. "Oh, why?"

"You've got to fulfill your destiny."

At that I sat up. "I thought you were my destiny." I ran my knuckles along her hip, little pieces of sand falling in their wake.

"Don't be silly," she said. "The game is speaking to you,

and you are not listening. It's telling you that you belong here."

"You getting mystical on me? Sounds like Hindu golf."

She sat up and spun around to face me. "I read *Hindu Golf* when I was a kid. I couldn't make any sense out of it." I actually didn't know there was any such book, but I didn't say so.

"What I'm talking about is that you refuse to recognize that golf is your whole life."

"Yeah, right," I said. "Especially when I play."

"What matters is the way you play."

"Bad is the way I play."

"Golf is how you connect to the human race. You don't see how important you are. You've touched hundreds of people."

"Let's just say, I like the touching part," I said, deciding to take charge of the moment. I took her by the shoulders and without force rolled her into some fresh sand.

So I sort of found the game in myself again because of Geegee. What I flirted with briefly, because of her, was real desire to play. Unfortunately, I did not find inside myself a championship player just waiting to be birthed. No, I began to play all right; that is, I could break 80 more or less regularly on a familiar course. I could appear in public for what I was, a teaching pro who understood and mastered to the level of his talent the mechanics of the game.

And thanks to Geegee and Harold Blaine, I discovered

I still had a little fire for golf. It all started when Geegee announced that we, she and I, were going to pair up for the State Mixed Best-Ball Championship. "You don't want me," I said. "Get yourself a player."

"It's going to be at Somerset," she said, her eyes announcing that she had made up her mind and I didn't have a choice. "It's a tight old course like this one. You have to be straight and smart. You can play it all right. And besides, I'll make the birdies.

The State Mixed Best-Ball Championship may sound like a big deal, but it is really just a two-day event played on a September weekend. Around a hundred twosomes played on Saturday, and we were cut to the low fifty and ties for Sunday. Most of the teams are amateurs, but here and there you will find a pro. The prizes aren't large enough to attract the hot-dog players from around the Twin Cities—and no pros drive in from outstate. No amateurs can win a merchandise prize valued at over $200, and if a pro should happen to be a member of a prize-winning team, he or she simply gets the value of the prize in cash. Second place, for instance, paid $125 and a silver medal with the Minnesota Golf Association emblem on one side.

Geegee was right that she would make the birdies. Saturday she made three, and we finished at 1 under, good enough to survive the cut but not better than twenty-fifth place. Still, only 5 under was leading, the cut was at 1 over, and anybody could realistically win.

So on Sunday, we tee off around midmorning, paired

with Harold Blaine and an aging former women's state champion from his club. I don't need to ask Blaine why he is playing for such small potatoes. His partner is a big deal in Minnesota women's amateur circles, her husband has tons of money, and Blaine has no choice. So there he is, his shirt collar up, his tee ball in fine shape, and his sweet Southern drawl just curling around his partner's ears. "Nice shot, Mildred. Way to hit that ball." I never heard him talk so much and comb his hair so little. He was obviously not taking this event seriously.

Blaine makes a move all his own on the front nine, making five birdies. On the 10th tee, we see by the clubhouse scoreboard that Blaine and his partner have a one-shot lead on the field. Even then the comb does not come out. I haven't hit a good shot yet, and Geegee and I have given back our lone red number and stand at even par.

Geegee walks over to me as we wait for Blaine to hit and pokes the butt end of her driver grip into my tummy. "Well, my friend," she whispers. "It's time for you to play a little. You must have spent too much time sleeping last night. Your blood's not awake yet."

As we move into the final nine, the wheels come off Blaine's game, his partner can't play a lick, and they give a couple of their shots back. But they are still in second place because nobody else in the field is doing anything much either. Evidently, the tightly wooded fairways and the lush, rolling terrain prove too much for the players.

Somerset is lush because it spends most of the summer

untouched. The membership is too old to play. The joke is that Somerset is such an old-money club that only those who can pay their dues with moldy money are accepted for membership.

Nobody is playing, that is, except Geegee, who starts spanking her irons into the greens for practically gimmes. She birdies three in a row and the longest putt is eight feet. On the 16th tee, Blaine says to her just loud enough for me to hear, "Too bad we're not partners. We'd be taking this tournament apart." Well, that just got under my skin. Blaine could just stick to his own damn partner. It's not my fault his game is coming apart.

On 16, a tabletop green surrounded by trees and grass bunkers, Geegee hits the fiercest 5-iron of her life and flies the green, taking herself out of the hole. "I don't care," she says to me, a joyous gurgle to her voice and her eyes as big as all outdoors. "Did you see how I put my hands into that thing? I can't hit a 5-iron that far."

"You can now," I say and walk over to give her a squeeze.

Geegee can't find her ball, and I'm looking at a thirty footer for par. I look at Harold Blaine, his upturned collar, the gray spit curl on his forehead. I feel a surge of energy in my forearms, and I drill the putt dead in the center of the hole. On 17, a 350-yard par 4, I hit the longest drive of my life, pinch a pitching wedge two feet from the hole, and tap in a birdie.

18 is a par 3. As I try to decide which club to use, Blaine

takes his comb out and starts to drag it through his hair. I feel a burst of elation because I've gotten to him, and I hit the meanest 7-iron of my life. The ball hits the hole on the fly and spins off the flagstick into a side bunker.

My streak is over. I take two from the bunker to get on the green. "Don't worry about it," Geegee says, and calmly knocks in her 40-footer for another birdie. We finish at five under, and I don't care where we stand with the field because we've beaten Blaine. As it is, we're the clubhouse leader for a couple hours until a late-afternoon group comes in at seven under. We finish second. Everybody at our club figures Geegee did all the work, and they think it was nice of her to take me along for this brief moment of glory.

After the mixed ball, I go down to spend a couple of weeks with my mother. When I get back I see Geegee only once. She tells me her grandparents have set things up for her at a club in Phoenix. She plans a rigorous winter of refining her game, and then from there she is going to try for the LPGA Tour, although she may have to play some mini-tours before she makes it. She has no doubt that she will make it.

I'm about to leave for my usual winter thing in Palm Springs, I tell her. I make it sound like I have a rather cushy position. The club is pretty swank, but actually I only work as a 1st-tee starter. At night I give lessons at a nearby driving range and hustle club repairs. We will have to get together in the desert, I say. She'll call, she says. Write, I say, in care of the club.

That winter I get two postcards about scores she is shooting and small events she is winning. I call twice about coming to see her, but she is too busy with her game. She is ecstatic about learning to play target golf and to putt the bumpy, dry greens of the desert. She is flying her irons farther and straighter now, and I ought to see her drive.

And so that was it.

I am back in the Cities in early March. I know Al assumes I will be working for him. He is just back from his winter home in Florida. He is unpacking boxes of stuff he's picked up at the winter PGA merchandise show. He's also very excited to tell me about how he won the Over-Sixty division at the PGA Club Pro Championship. He shot two 72s, best he's played in years, and nobody was within six shots of him.

"I don't think I'm coming back," I tell him. "I think I'll stay in the desert for the summer."

He throws a new sweater, nicely folded in its plastic bag, at me. The sweater hits my chest and falls to the floor. I don't stoop to pick it up.

"I've always wondered what the summers are like out there," I say, a bit lamely.

"Wonder, my butt." He raises his voice. It is the first time I've ever heard him raise his voice and I am surprised by its thin whine. "Let me tell you something. You're forty-three years old. It's time you quit bumming. I've got only a couple of years left here."

"I don't play well enough," I say.

"These people like you. They want a pro who will be in the shop when they come out to play. They've never been interested in a tournament player."

"I don't want a head job," I say.

"Want, my butt." Little bits of spittle fly out from his mouth. "You keep your nose clean here for a couple more years, and be around where they can see you a little bit more, and you'll get this job."

"I just don't want to be around here," I say a bit weakly. "I miss Geegee too much."

Al can't believe his ears. "You'd ruin your career because you can't stop mooning over that spoiled little brat?"

I start to walk out of the shop. "I wish your father were here," Al yells after me. "You need somebody to pound some sense into your head with a 5-iron."

I started hitting up the other pros in the Twin Cities for a teaching job. But nobody had anything. Everybody kept asking, What do you want to leave Al for? What I think happened was that the old rascal called everybody and told 'em to send me back to him if I showed up.

So I'm back working for Al. In spite of myself, I spend a little more time in the pro shop and around the 1st tee on weekends, joshing with the members. They use my first name and ask my advice about which club to hit when, and they seem to want to know what I think of this or that new theory. I guess Al's right that they like me.

Geegee's on the LPGA Tour now. Once in a while she's

close enough to the leaders to be on television. If I've got the Sunday shift in the shop, I'll have the TV on. She wraps the club around her neck regularly now, and she still putts with the ball back in her stance. She strides down the fairway like she's in charge of the world. Her eyes bore into the target and the corners of her mouth turn up. There's no doubt in her mind that this game was created just for her.

The LPGA Tour stopped in the Cities this year, and I gave some thought to going over as a spectator and maybe getting a chance to talk to Geegee. But I decided not to.

We did talk, though. Her grandparents brought her out to the club for dinner, and she came down to the shop. I happened to be alone. She looked the same, but she didn't seem as full of energy. Her body seemed not on the verge of action, but more relaxed. Maybe she had simply matured.

"There he is," she said in a sort of good-old-boy way when she came through the door.

"Hello, kid," I said.

She asked me how I was. "My life doesn't change," I said. "Although I'm playing more. Had a 34 on the back nine."

"1 under. Not bad."

"Very good for me," I said with a bit of a laugh. She stood on the other side of the showcase. We didn't touch. "Al's actually thinking about retiring. I think I may just put in for this job."

"These people like you. That's got to be worth something." Her tone was encouraging, her face bright, the edges of her mouth turned up. "Besides, you'd rather be at a golf course than any place in the universe."

"See you more and more on the TV now."

"I haven't won a tournament yet, but I will," she said. "I've got confidence."

"You always did," I said.

She left, and then she stuck her head back in the doorway. "I'm glad you're playing more," she said. Her eyes seemed to reassure me and her mouth was soft. And that was that.

I really am playing more than I did for many years. I can pretty much count on breaking 80 at home. This year the only tournament I played in was the State PGA, which is always thirty-six holes on a Monday in September. Al told me to play. "People around here have to start thinking of you as a class-A member of the profession," he said. Al really wants me to get this job when he retires. I'm not sure I care, but I guess I should care.

I think I really played in the PGA this year because it was held at Somerset. Uncle Thump was runner-up yet another time in the senior division. My scores wouldn't even have made money with the old guys. I didn't break 80 either round.

I would like to think it was because I couldn't hit a shot without thinking about Geegee. But the truth is, I think about Geegee all the time, anyway. I see her in what I've come to think of as our favorite moment. In the early mornings when the dew was still silver and she would come to the range and our eyes would meet for the first time that day and she would turn up the edges of her mouth in a smile that said everything was calm and good.

Or those times I would stay over and wake up before she did. I would lie on my elbow and watch her sleep, her lineless face seeming to be goodness itself. Then I think about the gurgles of pure joy she let out when she hit the golf ball. I see her swing, her strong hands releasing the club down the fairway, and I think about the way she storms the golf course without giving it a chance. I think about the way her tongue sticks out of the corner of her mouth when she concentrates, and the way her eyes go big when the ball lands exactly where she wants it to go.

In the mornings I wake up lonely. When I get to the range with the dew still glistening on the grass and sun warm on my early morning joints, I begin to feel the possibility of the day. When I was a kid the old man would send me out in the mornings with a whipping pole to whip the greens. It was a long pole with a board at the end and you pushed it across the green like a squeegee. It erased the dew and smeared the worm casts. After a while I got smarter and tied a length of hose to an electric cart and circled the green dragging the hose. It worked almost as well.

I have always loved the isolation of the early mornings

on golf courses. Everything smells clean and fresh and the grass squeaks underfoot. The course seems to be much more alive to me then, almost as if it is breathing.

Soon my pupils arrive and I set about doing what I feel best at, helping them achieve the joy that only comes from hitting the ball squarely on the clubface. I feel closest to my dad then, seeing myself as a small boy watching him move around a pupil patiently. He moves the club this way and that, explaining the importance of the shoulder under the chin, the crook in the right elbow, the way the hands release the power down the fairway.

9

Nothing
but
Birdies

I came down from the range at six o'clock on a Monday night in late summer and found Harold Blaine combing his hair in the pro-shop mirror. "What do you say, Pardner?" he said when I came into the shop.

"What are you doing here, Long Knock?" I answered. "No jackpot anywhere? It is Monday, ain't it?" I went behind the counter and checked the lesson book for the next day.

"That why you never show up at the jackpots?" he said. "Your dad would come play with us sometimes. He never got any of my money, but there were guys he could beat."

"That was my dad," I said. "He thought you guys were more fun than I do. I would rather teach on Mondays than tee it up and give all my money to you hot dogs. The only way I could beat anybody is over the head with a driver."

He put his comb in his pocket and came over to the counter. "That is true. You really can't play for sour buttermilk, can you?" He was matter-of-fact, no offense intended.

I was thinking of saying that the only times I'd played well, he'd been on the losing end. I was thinking of putting a lot of stress on "losing end," but he did not seem to be looking for a fight, so I replied in a rather self-deprecating way. "You've seen the only times I've played any good in recent years."

He paused at that. Then he stood, his eyes boring into me as if he couldn't make up his mind about something. I smiled back and waited for him to open his mouth. He ran his comb through his hair in slow, measured strokes.

Then he said, "It isn't dark yet. Let's go play a few holes."

"What for?"

"I need to talk to you." He looked around at the pro-shop walls. "Somewhere in the open."

We played 1, 2, 8, and 9. On the 1st tee, Blaine said, "I don't think I've ever played here." He waggled his driver and cracked the ball out to an easy flip wedge on the 380-yard

hole. I grunted and bunted down the middle. I hit a 7-iron to
the green. We both made pars. Blaine didn't speak.

On the 2nd hole, a downhill 5 par, I normally hit two
woods and a wedge. Blaine killed the tee ball, hit a 5-iron left
of the green, chipped up for easy birdie. My wedge lipped out
and Blaine batted the two-footer back to me. "You seem to
play all right," he said on the 8th tee.

"What are we doing out here?" I was tired and I let it
show. Blaine smirked. "Look," I said. "If you're going to talk,
talk." Blaine took his comb out. "And put that thing up your
ass." Blaine put a lazy smirk on his face, snorted, and ran the
comb through his hair.

"Some people called me out here to talk to me about
taking over as head pro when Al retires," he said. "You know
he's retiring next year?" Blaine teed up a ball. The 8th hole is
a short 4 par straight uphill. You need to fly it 280 to carry the
hill. Blaine's ball disappeared over the crest.

My heart was up in my throat. I thought that if I
decided I wanted Al's job, I could have it. I had not thought
about the possibility of having to fight for it. I cold-topped
my tee ball and it rolled to the base of the hill. "So why are
you talking to me?"

"I want to find out what you want to do. Al has been
telling the board you're the only one for the job. He thinks
they should just hand it to you. The people talking to me
think it would be nice to have a player in the job. Give the
club some recognition."

I put down another tee ball and knocked a wobbly draw

halfway up the hill. I decided not to tell Blaine that I wasn't sure whether I wanted the job. I pursed my lips, then moved into a gentle smirk. When I got to my ball, I hit it on the hosel. "I'll walk this one," I told him.

Blaine knocked in a ten-footer for a birdie. "A skin, a skin," he started chanting and dancing around the green. We weren't playing for money, and he couldn't possibly actually be that excited about making a birdie on such a short hole. I figured it was just nervous energy.

"I guess you can comb your hair, if you want to," I said.

Blaine took his ball out of the cup and threw it at me. I had never seen him in such a playful mood. "Look," he said. "I don't want to work in the pro shop. And I don't want to teach. So what I want to know is, if I get this job, are you going to stay here and work for me?"

"There ain't enough money on this earth," I said. "Let's play the 9th hole. I'm getting crabby. I need food."

"Listen," he said, "you've got enough of a following here so the only way I may be able to get the job is if I can tell certain members of the board that you've agreed to be my assistant."

"I'd have to do all the work. You don't know the first thing about being a golf pro. You'd never be around. You'd be playing in any and every tournament you could possibly get to."

"Got to," said Blaine in all earnestness. "In my case, if I can't make twenty grand playing in these small tournaments, it isn't worth being in the golf business."

"This may come as a great shock to you," I said. "But the business of golf is serving the public. It is staying home and promoting the enjoyment of the game for your members."

"That's other thing I need to know," he said, dropping a couple more balls on the green and stroking them toward the hole. "Do you think there's members with money enough so they'd sponsor me on the Winter Tour? I could get into the tournaments through the Monday qualifiers. The chances are slim, but I'm playing awfully well right now."

I couldn't believe I was hearing this. "Monday qualifiers? You're a glutton for punishment."

When my old man finally went out on the Winter Tour, the days of just any player showing up, paying his entry fee, and playing were over. The Tour had more players than it needed. You had to qualify on Monday to get into the tournament. Sometimes over three hundred club pros, golf bums, and starry-eyed kids with hot putters would compete for as few as four or five spots. Blaine was talking suicide.

I went over to the 9th tee and prepared to hit. Blaine scooped up his balls and followed. "What do you think? Would I find sponsors here?" I began to have serious doubts that Blaine was in sound mind. Al had not said anything to me about certain members wanting the club represented in tournaments.

"I don't know," I said. I hit a drive 240 in the right center. I should have no more than a 7- or 8-iron to the green. Blaine bombed one that was still twenty yards in the air where mine stopped rolling. "Hell of a hit," I said.

Blaine gave me a steely gaze. He started to reach for his comb, but held up. "You don't think I can get sponsors, and you won't work for me?"

I started walking. "I don't pay enough attention to the members to know if there are any big spenders here," I said. That was sort of a lie because there were members here who insisted on taking a lesson from me every week. "But you can count on me not working for you. I'd sell shoes first."

I hit a fat 7-iron that still had enough force to get the ball to the front of the green. Blaine's wedge hit on the back edge and bounced into the rough behind the green. Without so much as a good-bye, he walked across the green, picked up his ball, and kept walking toward the parking lot.

The next morning, my sister and I are having a bran muffin brunch in an all-glass restaurant somewhere in St. Paul. She's playing in the touring company of some big-deal Broadway show. They are downtown at the Ordway for two weeks.

"I play a sister," she says. "The part's not big, but the money's good."

"It might lead to something," I say, then tongue a raisin into the back of my lower front teeth.

"With you, things always have to lead to something," she says. "Actually, I hope not." She lifts a pat of butter and stares back and forth between it and her broken bran muffin. "I'm happy with my place in the theater. I get to be a star, and bang, I have a short career." She decides against the butter and drops it on the table with a splat of finality.

I can see she's been dieting. Her cheeks are lean, her forearms taut. "You're looking good," I say.

"Been working at it," she says. "Working with weights. Couple extra dance classes a week." I add her butter to the wad already melting on my muffin. She watches me with disdain. "I'm working on becoming a handsome woman." The snide edge to her voice is sharp.

"Heard from a couple of the members that the show is pretty good," I say. I don't say that they also said she was terrific.

"Why don't you come see," she says. "I can get you tickets."

I look around to see how I go about getting my coffee refilled. The sun is out and there's a harsh glare to everything in the café. "We made a deal a long time ago," I say. "You don't watch me play golf. I don't watch you act."

She looks hurt. I have evidently overjudged the degree of snide in her voice.

"Besides, I'd never find the theater. Took me forever to find this place."

"You don't know Grand Avenue?" She looks surprised, a sort of why-is-my-brother-so-unhip grimace on her face. "The company rents a house over on Summit. I wake up in this café every day."

I don't know what to say, so I stare at my coffee cup. She sneaks her fingers up on her muffin, but doesn't lift it to bite. She just sort of squeezes the side of it and pulls her fingers sharply away. "Besides, you don't play golf. Unless you started again."

"Oh, a little more than usual," I say. "I snuck out the other afternoon and made 36."

"Sneaked."

"Huh?"

"You sneaked out. 36. That's pretty good, isn't it? Sort of like the perfect tit?"

I don't know why, but I start telling her I'm playing more because of Geegee. And then I'm telling her about Geegee. It starts getting maudlin just as the waitress brings more coffee, and I stop talking.

My sister takes a huge bite of her muffin and chomps vigorously. "Let's see," she says finally. "This woman was a while ago? And you're still crying. God, how Midwestern."

"I wouldn't say I was crying exactly," I say. "I just sort of have this broken heart. I miss her. Things don't seem to mean as much."

"Like shooting 36?"

I don't say anything. My sister polishes off her muffin, drains her coffee, and draws a napkin across her lips. She crumples the napkin and lets it fall between us. I want to respond to this dramatic bit with "God, how New Yorkish," but I don't. Then she leans back in her chair.

"The only difference twixt love and grief," she intones for the neighborhood, "is want of wit."

"What the hell does that mean?" I ask.

"It means, big brother, you broke your own heart." She

stands up. "I gotta go. Come see the show." And she is gone.

I finish my coffee and worry about finding my way back to the course.

That afternoon, I go out just before dark by myself and play 1, 2, 8, and 9 like Geegee and I used to. The course is still and I get a chance to appreciate silence. On number 2, I start talking to the old man.

I had lazy-slapped the tee ball and was a couple yards into the right rough. It has been a rainy summer so the grass is thick. I knew I should have tried to catch the 7-wood square and been happy to have the ball roll as far as the flat in front of the green. But I keep thinking that one of these days I'm going to hit this green in two, so I took out the 3-wood.

I knew better but I went after it with a big lunge. I ripped a divot the size of a throw rug, and the ball squirted five or ten yards down the fairway. I looked over my shoulder and saw the old man standing just outside the rough's edge. He looked like he did in the early sixties, built close to the ground like a block of rock, his forearms bulging. "I don't know why you tried so hard to help me be a player," I said. "All I could ever do is think with my butt."

"I don't know either," he said.

I hit the 7-wood to the flat, essayed a high thump shot with a sand wedge four feet from the hole, and knocked in the putt with a firm hit-the-hole-or-the-highway stroke. "Made par," I said. The old man was sitting on the hogback behind the green. I walked over to him. "I can't decide if I want to be head pro here," I said. I threw down a couple of balls and putted back toward the hole. "I'm bothered by the way I play. I won't be going to the State PGA and turning in any kind of respectable scores. I don't know how the members will take to that."

The old man looked tired. His eyes were red and his massive frame was chipped and bruised around the edges, about the way he looked in the mid-seventies before it became all too clear how sick he was.

"Old Al's made a pile of money here," he said. "It's the kind of job I wished I would have gotten, and never did."

"You never wanted to live in a city," I said. "I didn't think you cared about money. Ain't no money in those dirt-water burgs you lived in."

The old man smiled, the smile pushing a little twinkle into his eyes. "Oh, there was money there. I just couldn't convince anybody to spend any of it."

I put the balls back in my pocket and wiggled the putter back and forth in front of my toes.

"Would have been a lot nicer for your mother if I'd ever gotten a job like this," the old man went on. "That Al, he could have retired yesterday and he still wouldn't have time to spend all his money."

I picked up my bag and walked over to the 8th tee. The old man was sitting on the bench. He was very old. His cheeks were waxy and his hair was all white. The skin fell away from the bottom of his eyes, showing a dull pink quick.

Nothing but Birdies

"You know," I said. "Geegee used to say I had to quit worrying about not being a good player. She said I had to listen to the game and let it decide my destiny. She said I had to let golf be the means of connecting with people, and when I did that, I would be content."

I took my driver out of the bag. "I just don't know if I could be content," I said. "She used to tell me I had to live with myself for who I was."

The old man just looked bewildered. He had an almost hurt look to his eye. "A lot of the early golf pros in Minnesota weren't good players," he said. "Hell, when they were looking for pros for the early courses, the members would meet immigrants in New York, and if a guy was a Scotsman, they hired him on the spot. Some of those guys didn't even play golf, but they learned soon enough. They had a good job and they wanted to keep it. They learned how to be of use to their members and the members appreciated them for it."

He came over and fished around in my clubs. He was younger and stronger again. The feel of golf clubs in his hands excited him. His hair was bluish gray and his wrists were thick as ankles. He took out a club. "I can play this hole with a 5-iron," he said.

I didn't pay much attention. "But then I don't know why I should care what Geegee thinks," I said. "At least all the people you helped get to be better players knew it." The old man fished a ball out of his pocket and set it on a tee. Then he stepped back and took several full practice swings. "I mean," I continued, "take Thump. If he would have taken the trouble to go big, he would not have said 'thank you' by walking out of your life."

The old man stepped up to the ball, and then paused to look back at me. He was young and cocksure like I had never seen him. His skin was smooth and his jaw stuck out. "Keep your eye on this one." And he hit it. He took a full pivot, his left foot practically off the ground, and the follow-through nearly flung him off the tee. The ball stayed in the air for over 200 yards. "You toe that club in, you can hit it for miles," he said, striding down the fairway.

I ran after him.

When he got to his ball, he hit a shot I've never seen before. He laid the 5-iron open, dropped his hands, stood still, and cut the damn thing like it was a sand wedge. The ball popped up like a rocket, carried the 120 yards or so to the green, and then fizzled, just sort of fell to the green like a feather, 3 feet from the cup. "A thump shot with a 5-iron from 120 yards?"

"It might have been 130," he said. "I used to practice that shot a lot when I was a kid. The only clubs I had were a cleek, a mashie, and a putter."

He walked up and chipped the ball into the hole. He didn't blade it or putt it. He chipped the ball off the clubface, the ball hopping in the air for about a foot and then rolling into the cup. "You don't need clubs," he said, smirking at me. "All you need is touch." He was a foot shorter and was wearing a white T-shirt and faded cotton pants rolled up over tennis shoes. A saucer of a softball cap was on his head. "We gotta make use of what daylight there is. You gonna play this game, or you gonna stand there with your teeth in your mouth?"

"You go ahead," I said.

He walked over to the 9th hole, teed it up, and split the fairway at 285. Only this time it was the old man in his prime. He was moving down the fairway at a lumbering bear step. In his hand was an old driver from the fifties, the Power Bilt model with the brass inset on the butt end. He was hot and he knew it, and he wanted to make birdies, nothing but birdies.